Centre for Baptist History and Heritage Studies
Occasional Papers Volume 10

'Church community is a gift of the Holy Spirit'

The spirituality of the Bruderhof community

Centre for Baptist History and Heritage Studies
Occasional Papers Volume 10

'Church community is a gift of the Holy Spirit'

The spirituality of the Bruderhof community

Ian M. Randall

Regent's Park College, Oxford

Regent's Park College is a Permanent Private Hall of The University of Oxford.

First published 2014

Centre for Baptist History and Heritage,
Regent's Park College,
Pusey Street,
Oxford,
OX1 2LB
(Regent's Park College is a Permanent Private Hall of
the University of Oxford.)
www.rpc.ox.ac.uk

19 18 17 16 15 14 13   7 6 5 4 3 2 1

British Library Cataloguing in Publication Data
A catalogue record for this book is available from the British Library

ISBN 978-1-907600-22-7

Front Cover Illustration:
Photograph of Eberhard Arnold
Courtesy of Bruderhof Historical Archives.

Typeset by Larry J. Kreitzer
Printed and bound in Great Britain
by Alphagraphics
www.alphagraphics.co.uk

'Church community is a gift of the Holy Spirit':
The spirituality of the Bruderhof community

The Bruderhof ('place of brothers') community traces its origins to the work of Eberhard Arnold, his wife Emmy, and her sister Else von Hollander in Germany in the early part of the twentieth century. The core group which formed the first community in 1920, in Sannerz, a village in the state of Hesse (north-east of Frankfurt), was shaped by a vision of a communal life which - as Eberhard Arnold put it - drew together 'reborn people who have accepted the life of the Sermon on the Mount'. These 'disciples of Jesus' were to be people who work, who 'radiate the spirit of Christ – people who witness for Christ with their entire being', and 'who give up everything to live simply and solely for love and for productive work'. The group wanted to testify 'that we are a church of Christ, a Lord's Supper fellowship.'[1] Almost a century later the Bruderhof consists of over 2,600 men, women, and children – families and single people - living in twenty-three intentional communities of differing sizes, most in Europe and North America. In 2012 the Bruderhof produced a document, *Foundations of Our Faith and Calling*, which (it explains) was 'the outcome of discussion and study within the Bruderhof communities about the basis of our life together'. There was an extended exercise of drafting and re-drafting of the text by Bruderhof members. This period of reflection concluded in June 2012 when all Bruderhof members world-wide adopted the text.[2] It was then published. This study examines the spirituality of the Bruderhof as expressed in its early period and in its current communal life as delineated in *Foundations*.

---

[1] Markus Baum, *Against the Wind: Eberhard Arnold and the Bruderhof* (Rifton, NY, and Robertsbridge: Plough Publishing House, 1998), p. 126.

[2] *Foundations of Our Faith and Calling* (Rifton, NY, and Robertsbridge: Plough Publishing House, 2012), p. vii. The sections of Foundations are: basis of our faith; our calling; heritage; church order; church actions; and life in community. I am grateful to the staff of the Bruderhof Historical Archive, who have assisted me in the course of this study.

Studies of the Bruderhof

In the 1960s and 1970s there was considerable interest in emerging intentional communities. Thomas Finger calls this 'the high point of countercultural experiments'.[3] The Bruderhof was one community that attracted attention. An important source that became available in this period was Emmy Arnold's account of her story, which she had gathered in bound volumes of notes. This was published in 1964. Emmy Arnold was then in her seventies and did not want what she knew of significant events and people connected especially with the Bruderhof's beginnings to be forgotten. The book was published with the title *Torches Together*,[4] and then in 1999 an expanded version was produced incorporating material from an unpublished diary of Emmy Arnold's and from other personal papers. The revised title was *A Joyful Pilgrimage: My Life in Community*. At the end of the book Emmy Arnold quoted from principles Eberhard had set out in 1925 regarding 'Why We Live in Community'. The final paragraph of the statement by Eberhard Arnold has this crucial reflection: 'Efforts to organize community in a human way can only result in ugly, lifeless caricatures. Only when we are empty and open to the Living One – to the Spirit – can he bring about the same life among us as he did among the early Christians.'[5] This pointed clearly to spirituality being at the heart of the story of the Bruderhof.

An example of someone who was drawn to the Bruderhof community after a long search in the 1940s and 1950s for authentic spirituality was Josef Ben-Eliezer. His story, published years later, was fittingly entitled, *My Search*.[6] He came from an Eastern European

---

[3] Thomas Finger, 'Review Essay: *Foundations of Our Faith and Calling*', *Mennonite Quarterly Review*, Vol. 87 (October 2013), p. 585.

[4] Emmy Arnold, *Torches Together* (Rifton, NY: Plough Publishing House, 1964).

[5] Emmy Arnold, *A Joyful Pilgrimage: My Life in Community*, (Rifton, NY: Plough Publishing House, 1999), pp. 168-9; cf. Eberhard Arnold, *Why We Live in Community* (Robertsbridge: Plough Publishing House, 1995), p. 13. An essay by Eberhard Arnold on 'Why We Live in Community' was published in *Die Wegwarte*, October/November 1925 and May/June 1925. It was republished in 1995.

[6] Josef Ben-Eliezer, *My Search* (Rifton, NY, and Robertsbridge: Plough Publishing House, 2004).

family living in Germany. The Nazi regime and the Second World War brought great suffering to the family and Josef Ben-Eliezer survived harrowing experiences in Siberia and elsewhere in the Russian territories, finally arriving in Israel. His vision was to fight for the cause of Israel in the aftermath of the holocaust, but he came to the conclusion that he could not promote this cause in a way that harmed others. Marxism attracted him but subsequently disappointed him. Towards the end of the 1950s, while in Germany, Ben-Eliezer heard of the Bruderhof and decided to visit them. Although he was not inclined towards Christianity at that stage, he was still intent on seeking answers that would address the problems of humanity and also address his personal need, since he acknowledged that 'I hadn't found what I was seeking after years and years'. After a time living in the Bruderhof, at one of the community meetings people began to share openly with each other. 'In that moment', said Ben-Eliezer, 'I felt the reality of the power of Christ who through the centuries has wanted to gather a people into unity, into brotherhood.'[7] His life and outlook were changed and the Bruderhof became his spiritual home, with his wider mission being increasingly directed to issues of peace and reconciliation.

Someone who attempted in the 1960s to interpret aspects of Bruderhof spirituality from a sociological perspective was Benjamin Zablocki, who was a long-term guest of the Woodcrest Bruderhof in New York in the late 1960s.[8] Zablocki's work, published in 1971, failed to take account, however, of the desire for change which Ben-Eliezer had found so powerfully present in Bruderhof spirituality. Zablocki interpreted the Bruderhof commitment to loving and serving God and others as something self-directed rather than other-directed; as 'the feeling that one's services are desperately needed'.[9] The strong emphasis in Bruderhof spirituality on the living presence of the Holy Spirit elicited the comment from Zablocki: 'The moral basis of the

---

[7] Ben-Eliezer, *My Search*, p. 92.

[8] Benjamin D. Zablocki, *The Joyful Community: An Account of the Bruderhof: A Communal Movement Now in Its Third Generation* (Chicago: University of Chicago Press, 1971). At the time when he wrote the book Zablocki was a graduate student at Johns Hopkins University, USA. He later became a Professor of Sociology at Rutgers University.

[9] Zablocki, *Joyful Community*, p. 29.

Bruderhof consists in whatever enables the community to contain the Holy Spirit.'[10] But Zablocki's idea of 'containing' the Spirit is not language used in the Bruderhof. Rather, Eberhard Arnold spoke in July 1935 of this understanding: 'The revelation of the Holy Spirit does not stop at any boundary... The Holy Spirit is a creative spirit.'[11] In similar vein, *Foundations* talks about the desire for community life 'to be inspired and led by the Holy Spirit'. The church as the body of Christ is described as 'no organization, but a living organism'.[12] Although the title of Zablocki's book was *The Joyful Community*, his interest was in the Bruderhof as a sociological phenomenon rather than a spiritual organism.

A fine doctoral thesis which included an examination of the early Bruderhof period was produced in 1973 by Antje Vollmer. This made use of significant primary material which illuminated the context in which the Bruderhof began. Vollmer offered an analysis of the various radical Christian movements active in Germany in the early twentieth century, especially the *Neuwerk* (New Work) movement, with which Eberhard Arnold was very involved in the early 1920s, together with two friends, Otto Herpel, a pastor in Lissberg, and Georg Flemmig, rector of a school in Schlüchtern.[13] It was at Sannerz, near Schlüchtern, that Arnold and a small group began, in 1920, to try to embody the principles of community to which they were committed. Although for Arnold there was 'new work' to do, he saw himself as standing in the line of those who had undertaken creative spiritual initiatives before. Indeed Vollmer cites a significant letter Arnold wrote in 1920 in which he drew attention to the area of Germany north of Frankfurt, noting the movements 'of far-reaching significance' that had existed there – specifically some near Büdingen, about twenty miles from Frankfurt. Arnold spoke of the presence there of the Cistercians in the thirteenth century, the later 'Inspirationists, Baptizers, and all manner of sectarians', and the Moravian

---

[10] Zablocki, *Joyful Community*, p. 57.

[11] Eberhard Arnold, *God's Revolution* (Rifton, NY, and Robertsbridge: Plough Publishing House), p. 43.

[12] *Foundations*, p. 29.

[13] Antje Vollmer, 'The *Neuwerk* Movement', Doctoral Thesis (Berlin, 1973), pp. 59-70. I am using a translation into English by Kathleen Hasenberg and Lotte Keiderling.

movement's very large settlement at Herrnhaag established in 1736 - in what Arnold called 'that enthusiastic, life-affirming epoch of the Moravian Church'. For Arnold these varied movements exhibited the spirituality he espoused, 'which combined revolutionary liberation with religious depth of spirit'.[14]

Another study of the Bruderhof undertaken in the 1970s was by John McKelvie Whitworth. He looked at the Shakers, the Oneida Community and the Bruderhof.[15] Whitworth recognised the ongoing importance of the teaching of Eberhard Arnold, although overstated his case by asserting that Arnold's teachings 'remain the canon of the Bruderhof'.[16] Eberhard Arnold himself directed people to many different authors throughout church history. To take one example, in his magnum opus, *Innerland*, which was ultimately published in its final form just after his death, Arnold spoke of the medieval mystic Meister Eckhart as one 'who in many ways knew the inner life as few others have done'.[17] In an attempt to examine Bruderhof spirituality, Whitworth, commenting on the Bruderhof claim that its community life was an 'organism' which was 'constantly evolving', looked at external features and argued that over several decades there had been no significant changes in Bruderhof communitarianism. However, his case for Bruderhof rigidity was rather undermined by his subsequent proposal that in the period when he wrote the communities seemed to him to be attempting to ignore Eberhard Arnold's insistence on evangelism.[18] With his sociological interests, Whitworth did not focus on the inner spiritual dynamics of the Bruderhof.

In 1996 Yaacov Oved produced what is the most comprehensive account of the Bruderhof to date, *The Witness of the Brothers*.[19] Oved, as a member of Kibbutz Palmachim since 1949, a former Professor in

---

[14] Eberhard Arnold to Hilde Hoppe in Marburg, 28 April, 1920, cited by Vollmer, 'The *Neuwerk* Movement', p. 60.

[15] John McKelvie Whitworth, *God's Blueprints. A Sociological Study of Three Utopian Sects* (London: Routledge & Kegan Paul Ltd, 1975).

[16] Whitworth, *God's Blueprints*, p. 177.

[17] Eberhard Arnold, *Innerland: A Guide into the Heart of the Gospel* (e-book, Rifton, NY, and Robertsbridge: Plough Publishing House, 2011), p. 15.

[18] Whitworth, *God's Blueprints*, pp. 181-2, 191.

[19] Yaacov Oved, *The Witness of the Brothers: A History of the Bruderhof* (New Brunswick, USA, and London: Transaction Publishers, 1996).

Tel Aviv University's history department, and an authority on communal movements, was well qualified to undertake detailed research and write this substantial book. He pointed out the significance of the continued existence of the Bruderhof over eight decades: 'From among the many German communities of the twenties [1920s], only the Bruderhof became a communal movement that has survived to this day.'[20] Oved highlighted the way in which the Bruderhof community was open and welcomed guests. Although it had gone through very difficult and divisive times, it was not a community that had closed in on itself. He quoted the Mennonite, Harold Bender, who spoke of the 'strong missionary spirit' in the early Bruderhof and who noted that in the course of one year (1930) the number of guests who came to the Bruderhof was 1,000 or more.[21] This number was to grow rapidly. As well as dealing fully with periods of community advance, Oved also gave sympathetic attention to the painful experiences of former members of the community. In the 1990s a non-partisan assessment was being made by Oved of community upheavals and power struggles that had happened a generation before. He spoke of the years 1959 to 1962 as 'years of great crisis, a dark period in Bruderhof history',[22] although arguably the 'dark period' was a consequence of problems that had built up previously.

By the time Oved was writing, the experiences of the Bruderhof, which included many internal spiritual challenges and struggles from the 1930s through to the 1980s, were being told by members and former members. The community had to leave Nazi Germany and it re-established itself in England in 1936, in Wiltshire, where it grew rapidly. But World War II broke out, and the British government told Bruderhof members that German nationals had to be interned. Instead, almost all emigrated, to Primavera (Spanish for spring), Paraguay. In 1961, in the midst of Oved's 'dark period', Primavera was dissolved. Many members left or were put out of the movement. Those who continued, now mainly in the USA, tried to find a way forward for the

---

[20] Oved, *Witness of the Brothers*, p. 33.

[21] Oved, *Witness of the Brothers*, p. 45, citing Harold Bender, 'The New Hutterite Bruderhof in Germany', included in *Brothers Unite* (Rifton, NY: Plough Publishing House, 1988), pp. 233-4.

[22] Oved, *Witness of the Brothers*, p. 207.

Bruderhof and in 1989 this story was told by Merrill Mow in *Torches Rekindled: The Bruderhof's Struggle for Renewal*. The title drew from *Torches Together*. There was a desire to acknowledge errors and failures of recent decades.[23] Former members of the Bruderhof also wanted to tell their stories, and these were published by Carrier Pigeon Press, which had been set up for that purpose. Memoirs included Roger Allain, *The Community that Failed* (1992), and Elizabeth Bohlken-Zumpe, a grand-daughter of Eberhard and Emmy Arnold, *Torches Extinguished* (1993).[24] Such stories formed the basis of a hostile book on the Bruderhof published in 2000 by Julius H. Rubin.[25] He was invited to visit Bruderhof communities, but declined. What he wanted was to interview Bruderhof patients with 'spiritual affliction and depression' and interview their physicians.[26] Given issues of confidentiality, this request is strange: it clearly could not be met.[27]

Other studies began to be produced in the 1990s which looked at specific aspects of the Bruderhof and at leading figures. Bob and Shirley Wagoner wrote *Community in Paraguay*.[28] Markus Baum produced a definitive study of Eberhard Arnold and the Bruderhof in the period up to Arnold's death in 1935. When the English language

---

[23] Merrill Mow, *Torches Rekindled* (Rifton, NY: Plough Publishing House, 1989).

[24] Roger Allain, *The Community that Failed* (San Francisco: Carrier Pigeon Press, 1992); Elizabeth Bohlken-Zumpe, *Torches Extinguished: Memories of a Communal Bruderhof Childhood in Paraguay, Europe and the USA* (San Francisco: Carrier Pigeon Press, 1993). The Press was set up by KIT, which is for ex-members of the Bruderhof. See also Nadine Moonje Pleil, *Free from Bondage* (1994); Belinda Manley, *Through Streets Broad and Narrow* (1995); Miriam Arnold Holmes, *Cast out in the World* (1997).

[25] Julius H. Rubin, *The Other Side of Joy: Religious Melancholy among the Bruderhof* (New York: Oxford University Press, 2000). Even before beginning his research, Rubin's interest was already in what he called 'religious melancholy'. See Julius H. Rubin, *Religious Melancholy and Protestant Experience in America* (New York: Oxford University Press, 1993).

[26] Rubin, *Other Side of Joy*, p. viii.

[27] Rubin's hostile treatment has been influential in some quarters. See, for example, Bonnie Price Lofton's uncritical acceptance in 'On the Survival of Mennonite Community in Modern-Day America: Lessons from History, Communities, and Artists', Drew University DLitt (2012), p. 31.

[28] Bob and Shirley Wagoner, *Community in Paraguay* (Rifton, N.Y., Lough Publishing House, 1991).

version, *Against the Wind*, was published in 1998, Jim Wallis of the
Sojourners Community wrote in the Foreword about the Bruderhof
movement as 'a vibrant community of faith from which we at
Sojourners have received great insight and strength over the years'.
He described how he had found in the Bruderhof 'a mutual respect, a
readiness to serve, and a joy in one another that has been born of
much faith and struggle'.[29] Wallis was pinpointing the importance of
Bruderhof spirituality. Faith and struggle were dominant themes in a
book published in 2004 by a community member, Peter Mommsen.
Entitled *Homage to a Broken Man*, it is a graphic account of the life of
Heinrich Arnold, one of the sons of Eberhard and Emmy, who for
twenty years – up to his death in 1982 – was pastor and elder of the
Bruderhof.[30] A wider-ranging study by Michael Tyldesley of
Manchester Metropolitan University in the same period looked at the
Kibbutz, the Bruderhof and the Integrierte Gemeinde, three communal
movements that trace their origins (at least in part) to the German
Youth Movements of the early twentieth century.[31] Finally, in 2009
and 2010, Emmy Barth, a senior archivist for the Bruderhof, made
very good use of the archives to produce important studies of the
community in Nazi Germany, until it was dissolved by the Nazis in
1937,[32] and of the early period in Paraguay.[33]

---

[29] Jim Wallis, 'Foreword' to Baum, *Against the Wind*, p. vii.

[30] Peter Mommsen, *Homage to a Broken Man* (Rifton, NY, and Robertsbridge:
Plough Publishing House, 2004). See also Richard Domer, Winifred Hildel and
John Hinde, *May They all Be One: The Life of Heini Arnold* (Rifton, NY: Plough
Publishing House, 1992).

[31] Michael Tyldesley, *No Heavenly Delusion?* (Liverpool: Liverpool University
Press, 2003), p. 65.

[32] Emmy Barth, *An Embassy Besieged* (Eugene, OR: Cascade Books, 2010).
Also Hans Meier, *Hans Meier Tells His Story: the Dissolution of the Rhoen
Bruderhof in Retrospect* (Rifton, N.Y.: Plough Publishing, 1979). Two Hutterites,
David Hofer and Michael Waldner, were visiting the Bruderhof in 1937 and helped
the community. Part of David Hofer's diary was published in the *Mennonite
Quarterly Review*. Robert Friedmann, ed., trans., 'Hutterites Revisit European
Homesteads: Excerpts from the Travel Diary of David Hofer', *MQR*, Vol. 33
(October 1959), p. 306.

[33] Emmy Barth, *No Lasting Home: A Year in the Paraguayan Wilderness*
(Rifton, NY, and Robertsbridge: Plough Publishing House, 2009).

Given the work done on Bruderhof history, *Foundations of our Faith and Calling* is not intended as a narrative of that history. It does trace crucial steps, beginning with the formation of the community in 1920. Eberhard and Emmy Arnold, and Else von Hollander, as they were confronted by 'mounting social injustice and the horrors of World War I', turned to Jesus' teachings, 'especially his Sermon on the Mount'. Through this, *Foundations* notes, 'they felt a call to radical discipleship: to give up everything for Christ.' The Sannerz group 'began to live in community of goods after the example of the first church in Jerusalem'. Young people were attracted and numbers grew to 150, but *Foundations* recounts how after Hitler's rise to power members became a target of National Socialist oppression: they 'refused to use the *Heil Hitler* greeting, serve in the German army, or accept a government teacher in their school'. In 1937 the secret police closed the community at gunpoint. *Foundations* continues: 'With the help of Mennonite, Quaker, and Catholic friends, all members were eventually reunited in England, and by 1940 the refugee community had doubled in size through an influx of English members.'[34] After moving from England to Paraguay they had twenty years 'as pioneer farmers in a harsh, unfamiliar climate, while also founding a hospital that served thousands of local patients'. *Foundations* concludes its summary – which does not attempt to deal with historical complexities – with the founding in 1954 of the first American Bruderhof community, in Rifton, New York, and the subsequent establishment of communities in the USA, UK, Germany (one in the original community house in Sannerz), Paraguay and Australia.[35]

Evangelical Spirituality: 'Christ's transforming love'

Eberhard Arnold, the main shaping force in the emergence of the Bruderhof, was born on 16 July 1883 near Königsberg. His mother, Elisabeth Arnold, née Voigt, was from a family of scholars, and his father, Carl Franklin Arnold, was the son of Swiss and American missionaries. Carl Arnold taught theology and philosophy and in 1888

---

[34] *Foundations*, pp. 21-22. I am grateful to Peter Mommsen for supplying me with material relating to British members, such as an unpublished autobiography and unpublished manuscript by Maureen Burn, *Truth Is Eternal*.

[35] *Foundations*, pp. 21-23.

was appointed Professor of Church History at Breslau University.[36] Although Carl Arnold read to his family from the daily texts of the Moravian Brethren, with their powerful evangelical spirituality,[37] Eberhard did not have any personal encounter with spiritual experiences that impressed him until he stayed - when almost sixteen – with his mother's cousin, Lisbeth, and her husband, Ernst Ferdinand Klein. Several things about Ernst Klein were significant. He had been a Lutheran pastor in a weavers' village and had taken up the cause of the workers in their struggles. This led to his removal by the Lutheran Church to another parish. Eberhard was struck by this and also by his uncle's 'courageous, joyful Christianity'. One memorable incident for Eberhard was when Ernst Klein warmly welcomed a Salvation Army member and called him 'brother'. Klein was keen to hear about the work of the Salvation Army among the poor in Berlin and Eberhard listened with fascination. Most Lutheran ministers of the time were dismissive of the Salvation Army and its spiritual commitments.[38]

After returning from his stay with his aunt and uncle, Eberhard embarked on an intense spiritual search. He would later tell Emmy his story: in October 1899, 'after a prolonged inner struggle', he visited a young pastor, having heard him speak. 'When he asked the pastor about the Holy Spirit', Emmy recorded, 'the pastor said, "It is just this Spirit that has led you here." So it happened that Eberhard experienced conversion.'[39] This was a classic evangelical conversion experience. Studies of evangelicalism in recent years have generally aligned themselves with David Bebbington's argument that evangelicals are those who stress conversion, the Bible, the cross, and activism.[40] These came together in Eberhard's experience. His conversion involved reading the Bible - John's gospel chapter 3, with a focus on being 'born again' (John 3:3). Jesus was now seen by him as God's Son, and as his Saviour and Redeemer (John 3:16). Arnold

---

[36] Baum, *Against the Wind*, pp. 2-3.

[37] I.M. Randall, 'Christ comes to the heart: Moravian influence on the shaping of evangelical spirituality', *Journal of European Baptist Studies*, Vol. 6, No. 3 (2006), pp. 5-23.

[38] Baum, *Against the Wind*, p. 8.

[39] Emmy Arnold, *Joyful Pilgrimage*, p. 2.

[40] D.W. Bebbington, *Evangelicalism in Modern Britain: A History from the 1730s to the 1980s* (London: Routledge, 1995), pp. 2-17.

continued to stress the Bible, writing of it in *Innerland* as the only book 'that can satisfy the inner life and fill the heart'.[41] As evidence of continued emphasis on the cross, he spoke of how 'the proclamation of the cross becomes a divine power; coming from the heart of God' and he quoted the 'rule and method' of the Moravian leader, Count Zinzendorf, 'to make the glorious Lamb everything'.[42] Arnold's activism was highlighted when at age eighteen he began to preach in Salvation Army circles. He described speaking some years later at 'a powerfully blessed Salvation Army meeting': he had 'seldom experienced anything like it'.[43] Christian spirituality can be seen as concerned with the conjunction of theology, communion with God and practical Christianity.[44] Desire for this conjunction to be achieved in an authentic way was at the heart of Eberhard Arnold's commitment from 1899 onwards.

Foundations speaks of people experiencing 'Christ's transforming love'.[45] Following his own experience of this transformation, Arnold began to make contact with students and others meeting in small groups for worship, Bible study and fellowship. One Bible study group which was established and to which Arnold gave energy soon grew to fifty students. In 1901 Eberhard began to take an interest in movements of renewal and change in church history, especially the sixteenth-century Reformation. This was something his father encouraged. The movement that most attracted Eberhard was radical: Anabaptism. Although there were differences between different Anabaptist groups, the common position for nearly all was re-baptism - based on the rejection of the validity of infant baptism - and rejection of a state church. As Arnold Snyder puts it, to be an Anabaptist was to make 'a faith decision that directly confronted and challenged the social, religious, and political status quo'.[46] Through his father,

---

[41] Arnold, *Innerland*, p. 39.

[42] Arnold, *Innerland*, p. 184.

[43] Eberhard Arnold to Emmy von Hollander [hereafter, Eberhard and Emmy], 29-30 June 1907, *Love Letters*, (Plough Publishing House: Rifton, NY, and Robertsbridge, 2007), pp. 100-1; Emmy Arnold, *Joyful Pilgrimage*, p. 3.

[44] P. Sheldrake, *Spirituality and History* (London: SPCK, 1991), p. 52.

[45] *Foundations*, p. 8.

[46] C. A. Snyder, *Anabaptist History and Theology: An Introduction* (Kitchener, Ontario: Pandora Press, 1995), p. 2.

Eberhard became aware of Johann Loserth, an Austrian Professor who had researched a communitarian Anabaptist movement led by Jakob Hutter. Eberhard read Loserth's volumes on Anabaptism in the Tyrol, in his father's library, and he was attracted by Loserth's description of Anabaptists as 'good, faithful people with a pure way of life and love of Jesus'. Eberhard found here a movement that spoke to him about how to follow Jesus. It also raised queries in his mind about the Lutheran state church.[47]

In 1905 Eberhard Arnold began as a student at Breslau University, studying theology. He immediately became part of the Student Christian Movement (SCM) and attended an SCM conference in that year at which the speakers included Karl Heim, later a professor of Dogmatics at Münster and Tübingen, and R.A. Torrey, an American evangelist who undertook evangelistic campaigns similar to those of D.L. Moody. Torrey spoke at the conference of 'the personal experience of the Spirit's power' and of the experience of 'baptism by the Spirit'. Later Eberhard recommended Torrey's work on 'fullness of power'.[48] Eberhard had received an invitation from General William Booth to serve in the Salvation Army, but he felt his spiritual home was to be with the SCM and the YMCA. He was elected chairman of the Halle branch of the SCM and in his inaugural address to the branch he set out in powerful terms his vision, one that was not his own construction but expressed the heart of evangelical spirituality: 'We do not want to be or become an isolated sect, but rather a missionizing power for all groups in our universities. We do not want to set up a party or direction within Christianity, but rather to unite Christians of every hue under the banner of Jesus…Only Jesus! That is the motto of our movement. We know we do not belong to ourselves any longer, but that he has redeemed us to God by his blood.'[49]

Eberhard Arnold's reference to uniting 'Christians of every hue under the banner of Jesus' reflected the pan-denominational

---

[47] Eberhard Arnold, *Aus dem Worte Gottes*, cited by Baum, *Against the Wind*, pp. 14-15.

[48] Eberhard Arnold to Emmy von Hollander, 9 April 1907, in Bruderhof Historical Archive [BHA], cited by Baum, *Against the Wind*, p. 19.

[49] Text of address, Arnold to Emmy von Hollander, 1 July 1907, BHA, cited by Baum, *Against the Wind*, p. 23.

spirituality of the student body, the SCM, and also, more broadly, of the Evangelical Alliance. From its origins in London in 1846 the Evangelical Alliance wished to promote unity among Christians and across national boundaries. A key figure in the international impetus was a Swiss-American, Philip Schaff, a Professor at Union Theological Seminary, New York. Schaff's ecumenical vision derived from Lutheran and Reformed connections and he envisaged the possible ultimate coming together of Catholic, Protestant and Orthodox Churches.[50] In the 1890s British Evangelical Alliance representatives such as the leading Baptist, F.B. Meyer, attended German Evangelical Alliance conferences at Bad Blankenburg, and in 1899 Meyer spoke of the remarkable *Gemeinschaftsbewegung* or 'Fellowship meeting' movement in Lutheranism, wondering if this would revive or split the Church.[51] For Eberhard Arnold, the transdenominational 'Fellowship' groups and the Alliance provided spiritual nourishment. In 1907 Halle saw a powerful revival movement. This had links with wider revival in Europe, drawing from the (1904-05) Welsh Revival.[52] In Halle there was a revival Fellowship on the Alte Promenade (now Paracelsus-Strasse), meeting in the reconstructed studio of a painter. Arnold seems to have co-founded this Fellowship. Links with the Evangelical Alliance led to Arnold publishing in their magazine and speaking at the Bad Blankenburg conference in 1907.[53] Arnold also held evangelistic meetings in Halle, Berlin, Hamburg and Erfurt with the lawyer-evangelist Ludwig von Gerdtell, founder of the European Evangelistic

---

[50] Ian Randall and David Hilborn, *One Body in Christ: The History and Significance of the Evangelical Alliance* (Carlisle: Paternoster Press, 2001), p. 138; N.M. Railton, *No North Sea: The Anglo-German Evangelical Network in the Middle of the Nineteenth Century* (Leiden: Brill, 2000), pp. 183-4.

[51] Minutes of the Executive Council of the Evangelical Alliance, 11 July 1895; *Evangelical Alliance Quarterly*, 2 October 1899, p. 20.

[52] Emmy Arnold spoke of revivals in America, Norway, Sweden, Wales and Finland. Emmy to Eberhard, 7 August and 9 August 1907. A key linking figure was Eva von Tiele-Winckler of the Friedenshort (Refuge of Peace), who was working among the poor. She and some friends visited Wales to experience the awakening.

[53] Baum, *Against the Wind*, pp. 25-6. See Appendix 1.

Society, and Arnold contributed an article, 'Work among the educated', to a series by von Gerdtell on 'world-view issues'.[54]

The year 1907 was of even greater significance for Eberhard because he met Emmy von Hollander. She was originally from Riga, Latvia, from a distinguished family, and in 1905 was working as a probationer nurse at the Halle Deaconess House. On 4 March 1907 Emmy and her sisters Else and Monika heard Eberhard Arnold speaking at a meeting. He drew from Hebrews chapter 10: 'Since we have confidence to enter the sanctuary by the blood of Jesus... let us draw near with a true heart in full assurance of faith.' Emmy described how she felt 'the call to life-long discipleship'.[55] Soon Eberhard and Emmy became engaged, and for periods of time exchanged almost daily letters.[56] The relationship of conversion to baptism became an issue in their correspondence. In May 1907 Eberhard saw infant baptism as 'willed by Jesus and God'.[57] A month later he commented: 'The agitation over baptism... cannot be of the Holy Spirit.'[58] Eberhard and Emmy never approached the Bible 'simply as an abstracted text', but 'as something to be read under the guidance of the Holy Spirit'.[59] Serious study of the Bible and prayer led Eberhard to a change of mind: on 4 September 1907 he told Emmy that he had 'been convinced by God, with quiet and sober biblical certainty, that baptism of believers alone is justified'.[60] Eberhard thought about joining a Baptist Church, 'since their beliefs, more so than their way of life, correspond so closely with my ideal'. He wrote about being 'deeply refreshed' by reading *All of Grace* by the leading Baptist pastor, C.H. Spurgeon. But Emmy pointed out that baptism was demanded for every Baptist member. This, for Eberhard, made

---

[54] Ludwig von Gerdtell, ed., *Burning world-view issues for thinking modern people*, No. 4 (1907), cited by Vollmer, 'The *Neuwerk* Movement', p. 53.

[55] Emmy Arnold, *Joyful Pilgrimage*, p. 10.

[56] The letters they exchanged during their engagement were put together by Emmy in nine volumes.

[57] Eberhard to Emmy, 11 May 1907, *Love Letters*, p. 56.

[58] Eberhard to Emmy, 29-30 June 1907, *Love Letters*, p. 102.

[59] I am indebted to Professor John Briggs for this comment on Eberhard and Emmy.

[60] Baum, *Against the Wind*, pp. 33-5. Eberhard to Emmy, 6 September 1907, *Love Letters*, pp. 132-3.

Baptists sectarian.[61] Baptist approaches to baptism and church membership were in line with the practice of the Anabaptists, but Arnold was more attracted by the perspective of von Gerdtell, who argued that the baptism of a believer should not mean 'sectarian separation'.[62]

Eberhard Arnold's baptismal quest was part of his concern to follow the teaching of Jesus. Speaking of baptism as something an individual should choose for himself or herself, Arnold insisted that the central issue was 'Jesus only! Jesus as God and Lord, whatever it may cost.'[63] Arnold was also stressing the need to live out the teaching Sermon on the Mount. In a letter to Emmy in 1907 he wrote about the interest among evangelicals in the Second Coming of Christ – the idea of 'the rapture': 'Testify resolutely to Jesus' will', he urged Emmy, and added: 'My feeling is that Matthew 5:13–16 is more important for you than the rapture: "You are the salt of the earth...".'[64] Arnold was disqualified in 1908 from sitting his doctoral examinations in theology because he had made known that he was not willing to be a pastor in the Lutheran Church and was going to be baptised as a believer. Else von Hollander had announced in 1907 her wish to be baptised as a believer, which the family viewed as social suicide.[65] Else was baptised in August 1908 and in October Eberhard - against the background of strong opposition from his family - was baptised in Halle, in the White Elster River, by a Leipzig doctor, Gotthelf Müller.[66] Emmy's baptism took place in December, in the Blücher Fellowship in Berlin. She was baptised by Pastor Köhler, a leader of the Fellowship and of an Evangelical Alliance Bible School.[67] Eberhard completed a philosophy thesis, on Friedrich

---

[61] Eberhard to Emmy, 16 Sept 1907, BHA, cited by Baum, *Against the Wind*, p. 38. See also Eberhard to Emmy, 14 November 1907, *Love Letters*, p. 166.

[62] John Howard Yoder, 'Introduction', Eberhard Arnold, *God's Revolution: Justice, Community, and the Coming Kingdom* (Rifton, NY, and Robertsbridge: Plough Publishing House, 1997), p. xx.

[63] Baum, *Against the Wind*, p. 38.

[64] Eberhard to Emmy, 1 May 1907, *Love Letters*, p. 49.

[65] Emmy to Eberhard, 12 May 1907, *Love Letters*, p. 57.

[66] Emmy to Eberhard, 19 October 1908, BHA, cited by Baum, *Against the Wind*, p. 49.

[67] Emmy Arnold, *Aus unserem Leben* (unpublished memoirs), BHA, cited by Baum, *Against the Wind*, p. 51.

Nietzsche, in 1909, and graduated 'Summa cum laude'. Soon Eberhard and Emmy were married and set up home in Leipzig.[68]

The lives of the young couple were full, with many meetings being addressed, people being cared for and considerable travelling undertaken. However, in the midst of all this evangelical activism a perspective was to open up which would add new dimensions to their evangelical spirituality. There were Baptists and other evangelicals in this period, such as Walter Rauschenbusch, an influential 'social gospel' advocate, who were looking to Anabaptist views for inspiration in a quest for social justice.[69] Rauschenbusch, whose ministry was undertaken in America, had 'warm ties' with the European Christian socialist, Hermann Kutter, who was a Lutheran pastor in Zürich.[70] The British Baptist author, Richard Heath, who translated works by Kutter into English under the title *Social Democracy*, was also admired by Rauschenbusch. Heath's work wedded an Anabaptist ideal of church as community 'to the goal of creating a democratic socialist society'.[71] In 1910 Eberhard Arnold read the book *They Must!* by Kutter,[72] and Arnold was deeply impressed by Kutter's positive presentation of Christian socialism. Another influence on Arnold was the social anarchist and pacifist, Gustav Landauer. From 1913 to 1917, Arnold wrestled with his feeling that 'purely personal Christianity' was inadequate and that Christ's work must be expressed in 'tangible ways'.[73]

---

[68] Emmy Arnold, *Joyful Pilgrimage*, pp. 13-15.

[69] Christopher Evans, *The Kingdom is Always but Coming: A life of Walter Rauschenbusch* (Grand Rapids: Eerdmans, 2004), p. 155.

[70] Paul Minus, *Walter Rauschenbusch, American Reformer* (New York, NY: Macmillan, 1988), p. 163.

[71] Richard Heath, *Anabaptism* (London: Alexander and Shepheard, 1895), p. 193. See J.H.Y. Briggs, 'Richard Heath, 1831–1912: From Suburban Baptist to Radical Discipleship by Way of Anabaptism', in J.H.Y. Briggs and A.R. Cross, eds., *Freedom and the Powers* (Didcot: The Baptist Historical Society, 2014), pp. 69-84.

[72] Theo Hobson, *Reinventing Liberal Christianity* (Grand Rapids, Mich.: Eerdmans, 2013), p. 230.

[73] Eberhard Arnold, *Salt and Light: Living the Sermon on the Mount* (Rifton, NY, and Robertsbridge: Plough Publishing House, 1998), pp. xiv-xv. Foreword by Jürgen Moltmann.

Foundations has the same evangelical emphases as those to be found in Eberhard Arnold. The first article in *Foundations* speaks of the Bruderhof community's life as 'founded on Jesus, the Christ and son of God. We desire to love him, to follow him, to obey his commandments, and to testify in word and deed to the coming of his kingdom here on earth', and the second states: 'Our faith is grounded in the Bible, the authoritative witness to the living Word of God. Through the Holy Spirit, we seek to be guided in all things by the Old and New Testaments'.[74] The biblicism of *Foundations* is seen in its many biblical references. *Foundations* also expounds a robust crucicentrism:

> By taking suffering and death upon himself, he [Christ] atoned for our sins and the sins of the whole world. His cross is the only place we can be forgiven and find peace with God and one another. The cross is the means of our personal salvation, but it is also more: it has cosmic significance. Here Christ overcomes all powers of evil and enmity, fulfills the justice of God, and reconciles the whole universe to himself.[75]

Conversionism is also clearly evident. 'Full surrender to Christ' is seen as the basis of discipleship and means 'repentance and conversion, of which baptism is the sign'.[76] Later *Foundations* speaks of true repentance as 'a gift of God', which is 'recognizable by a remorseful and contrite heart, a desire to confess one's sins, and a changed life that shows fruits of a new spirit'.[77] Finally, active mission is encouraged. The church community 'sends out brothers and sisters to proclaim the gospel' and in doing so 'our prayer is that the original apostolic commission might become a reality today as it was in New Testament times: for Christ's messengers to be equipped with

---

[74] *Foundations*, p. 1.

[75] *Foundations*, p. 8. Finger, 'Review Essay', p. 589, suggests that this view of the cross aligns itself with more radical, socially concerned theology. It is however, no less evangelical because of that. See John Stott on 'the objective decisive victory of the Lamb over all the powers of darkness which He won when He shed His blood on the cross.' John Stott, *The Cross of Christ* (Downers Grove, Ill.: InterVarsity, 1986), p. 251.

[76] *Foundations*, p. 30.

[77] *Foundations*, p. 51.

the full authority of the Spirit, going into all the world to invite people to the great feast of the kingdom of God'.[78] The heart of evangelical spirituality is personal relationship with Christ,[79] and *Foundations* talks unequivocally of the importance of 'a living relationship with Christ'. Without personal connection with Christ, *Foundations* maintains, 'church community will wither away'.[80]

'Community of goods'

In the spring of 1913, after Eberhard had held meetings in Halle, he became seriously ill with tuberculosis and for the sake of his health he and Emmy and their children – at that time Emi-Margret and Eberhard, later to be joined by Heinrich, Hans-Hermann and Monika - moved to the Tyrol. This was an area where Anabaptist communities had been present in the early sixteenth century, and the Arnolds gave greater attention to Anabaptist figures such as Hans Denck, Balthasar Hubmaier and Jakob Hutter.[81] Many Anabaptists, including the Mennonites (called after Menno Simons), encouraged mutual aid within Christian communities, but it was the Hutterites (called after Hutter) who implemented community of goods.[82] Because of fierce persecution of the Anabaptists in 1525-30, many of those in Swiss, Tyrolean and south German areas fled to Moravia. Hutter, who arrived in Moravia in 1529, led a group that formed a church. They found the basis for their espousal of community of goods in many Old and New Testament verses. The basic texts were in Acts, with the practices of the church in Jerusalem. In the gospels, the parable of the rich man and Lazarus addressed the issue of holding property in the context of

---

[78] *Foundations*, p. 18.

[79] I have developed this in I.M. Randall, *What a Friend we have in Jesus* (London: DLT, 2005).

[80] *Foundations*, p. 77.

[81] Emmy, *Joyful Pilgrimage*, pp. 17-18.

[82] For the early Hutterites see Hutterian Brethren, ed., *The Chronicle of the Hutterian Brethren, Volume I* (Rifton, NY: Plough Publishing House, 1987); Hans Fischer, *Jakob Huter* (Newton, Kan.: Mennonite Publication Office, 1956); Werner Packull, *Hutterite Beginnings: Communitarian Experiments during the Reformation* (Baltimore: The Johns Hopkins University Press, 1995); and James M. Stayer, *The German Peasants' War and Anabaptist Community of Goods* (Montreal: McGill-Queen's University Press, 1991).

human suffering.[83] Hutterites saw themselves as part of a spiritual tradition: they pointed to church fathers who praised giving away possessions, and to denunciations of selfishness in Thomas à Kempis' *The Imitation of Christ*.[84] Hutter's successors, especially Peter Walpot and Peter Riedemann, created rules for community of goods and saw community as normative for the church.[85] In his *Confession of Faith,* Riedemann argued that the one who is freed from 'created things' can grasp 'what is true and divine'.[86]

Eberhard and Emmy Arnold were fascinated by the Anabaptist stories. They were in the area not only from where Hutter originated but also to which he returned in spring 1535. Having been betrayed by a fellow-Anabaptist, he was executed in Innsbruck in February 1536. Local archives had preserved court records relating to Hutter and other Anabaptists, and these were studied by the Arnolds.[87] At the time they did not know that the Hutterites still existed as communities in America. Although there have been suggestions that Eberhard Arnold came to know about the American Hutterites in the mid-1920s through the scholar Robert Friedmann, it has been established by Markus Baum that Arnold's first awareness came in 1921, through a letter from J.G. Evert, a Mennonite and a philology professor at Tabor College, Kansas.[88] Eberhard Arnold later made an extended visit to the Hutterite communities in America, and the Bruderhof belonged to the Hutterites from 1930 to 1955 and 1974 to 1995.[89] Arnold never lost the sense of having encountered something powerful in his discovery of early Hutterite life. After his return from America in 1931 he stated: 'The difference between our Bruderhof and American

---

[83] L. Verduin, *The Reformers and Their Stepchildren* (Grand Rapids: William B. Eerdmans, 1964), p. 22.

[84] Stayer, *German Peasants' War*, p. 431; J.P. Klassen, *The Economics of Anabaptists* (The Hague: Mouton and Co., 1964), p. 84.

[85] Stayer, *German Peasants' War*, p. 144.

[86] Peter Riedemann, *Confession of Faith* (Rifton, NY: Plough Publishing House, 1970), p. 90.

[87] Baum, *Against the Wind*, p. 73.

[88] Baum, *Against the Wind*, p. 134.

[89] For a full account of the sometimes stormy relationship, see Rod Janzen, 'The Hutterites and the Bruderhof: The Relationship between an Old Older Religious Society and a Twentieth-Century Communal Group', *MQR*, Vol. 79 (October 2005), pp. 505-44.

Hutterism consists largely of this: We seek to find our spiritual nourishment and foundation in the first and the second Hutterian periods... whereas in the American communities it is the later period (seventeenth century) that serves that purpose... [we] want to become Hutterian in the sense of those first sixty years, from 1528-1589.'[90]

Eberhard Arnold became increasingly concerned to see how the community life of the Early Church could be embodied. As he travelled and lectured, what he said was received by many with enthusiasm, although rejected by others. A significant youth conference was held in Schlüchtern, north-east of Frankfurt, at Pentecost 1920. Schlüchtern was where Georg Flemmig had been seeking to pioneer an 'Early Church' movement that had attracted Eberhard, Emmy and Else. At the conference, Eberhard took up the themes of 'The Mystery of the Early Church', and the spirit of Pentecost.[91] Following the conference, Eberhard and Emmy and some young people walked to the nearby village of Sannerz, to make enquires about a house and fields which might be suitable for a community. After weeks of discussion a rental agreement for ten years was signed. The working community life which the Arnolds had envisaged took concrete form.[92] Initially the core group was small: Eberhard and Emmy, now with five children, Else, and a few others, including Suse Hungar, a Salvation Army captain and teacher. There were many visitors, however, and despite severe challenges, including a serious division in 1922, the community gradually grew, supporting itself by agriculture and publishing. In 1926, in what Eberhard called 'a step of faith',[93] a neglected farm in the Rhön, a few miles from Sannerz, was purchased. It was the largest of several farms in the Rhön, in the Fulda district of Hesse. Between 1926 and 1930 the community grew from 30 to 70, with baptisms taking place. In a letter

---

[90] Irmgard Keiderling to Else von Hollander, 15 May 1931, cited by Baum, p. 207; cf. *Brothers Unite*, p. 249.

[91] 'Das Geheimnis der Urgemeinde', printed in *Das Neue Werk*, No. 20–21, p. 160; cf. Baum, *Against the Wind*, p. 123

[92] Baum, *Against the Wind*, p. 123. Emmy Arnold, *Joyful Pilgrimage*, pp. 36-40.

[93] Eberhard read A.T. Pierson's biography of George Müller in 1908 and wrote to Emmy that never before had 'praying in faith' become so real to him. He believed God wanted him to live 'from faith alone'. Eberhard to Emmy, 31 August 1908, *Love Letters*, p. 232.

in 1926 Arnold spoke of the community as a 'Bruderhof'.[94] By this time Arnold had obtained from Friedmann the address of Elias Walter, a Hutterite elder in North America, and he wrote him a long letter. In the meantime the Rhön community was finding and copying Anabaptist documents, for example a 355-page manuscript with court records concerning Peter Riedemann.[95]

As well as opening up correspondence with Walter, Arnold contacted two American Mennonite leaders and historians, John Horsch and his son-in-law Harold Bender. In a letter in January 1928 he explained to Horsch that the spiritual roots of the Rhön Bruderhof went back to many different sources, including revival movements in Germany; the Baptists and the Salvation Army; Quakers, with their peace witness; youth movements, with their love of nature, which Arnold greatly valued; and workers' movements. Arnold told Horsch about a book he had written on the early Christians which illuminated the 'spiritual life of our Bruderhof' as lived in the modern world. He also wanted to discuss with Horsch and others 'the task of mission and evangelizing today', commenting that he had been unable to find among Hutterite communities in America any mission 'comparable to what happened so powerfully in Moravia' through early Hutterites.[96] At the end of 1928 Arnold was in correspondence with Elias Walter. Arnold expressed the determination of the Rhön Bruderhof to join the Hutterites. He also discussed baptism, affirming the view of Andreas Ehrenpreis, a seventeenth-century Hutterite bishop, that the mode of baptism – immersion or pouring – should not be a divisive issue. Arnold had been speaking to a gathering of Baptist pastors and was happy to tell Walter they accepted that community of goods was not 'unbiblical or fanatical' but was present in the early Jerusalem church.[97]

By this time the Rhön community was making plans for Arnold to visit the American Hutterite communities and unite the Rhön Bruderhof with them. This was not straightforward. Elias Walter explained that the American Hutterites were divided into three groups

---

[94] Baum, *Against the Wind*, pp. 168-70.

[95] Baum, *Against the Wind*, p. 180.

[96] Eberhard Arnold to John Horsch, 9 January 1928, in *Brothers Unite*, p. 2.

[97] Eberhard Arnold to Elias Walter, 6 November 1928, in *Brothers Unite*, pp. 6-9.

- in South Dakota, Manitoba, and Alberta. Arnold wrote to them all. He also wrote to Robert Friedmann, in June 1929, expressing his enthusiasm for the way Hutterite communities put faith into action, 'so that here and now in the practical, communal church life the kingdom of God is shown as justice, peace, and joy in the Holy Spirit (Romans 14:17)'.[98] In similar tones, Arnold wrote to John Horsch about 'centuries-old tradition, which all too easily brings a gradual loss of the first zeal of faith, love, and personal experience of Christ', but in the case of the Hutterites Arnold believed that 'their prayer for the Holy Spirit proves that the living breath of truth is not and cannot be extinguished.'[99] The Rhön community re-affirmed in August 1929 'by unanimous Brotherhood decision' Arnold's visit to America.[100] During this period Arnold travelled to Austria to discuss with Professor Loserth editing and publishing old Hutterite works, and gave lectures at Friedmann's 'Tolstoy Club' in Vienna. Arnold also travelled to Sabatisch (Sobotište) and Velké Leváre (both in present-day Slovakia), which were early Hutterite settlements. He met descendants of the Anabaptists and saw old Hutterian sites. Among his finds was a valuable Hutterian document of 1652 in the Moravian Herrnhut archives.[101]

Although the main focus of the Rhön Bruderhof was unity with Hutterite communities, two of Arnold's Mennonite contacts, John Horsch and Harold Bender, gave significant encouragement to Arnold before and during his American trip. Just before leaving for America, Arnold wrote to Bender on 20 May 1930 to thank him for visiting the Rhön community. Arnold expressed the gratitude of the community that Bender had been 'given the power and insight to realize that, in spite of our special way of expressing it, the only single thing of importance for us is representing the true and real gospel.' Arnold added that the Rhön Bruderhof was not part of those movements that

---

[98] Eberhard Arnold to Robert Friedmann, 6 June 1929, in *Brothers Unite*, p. 26.

[99] Eberhard Arnold to John Horsch, 14 September to 9 October 1929, in *Brothers Unite*, p. 43.

[100] Report of a Meeting of the Brotherhood and Novices at the Rhön Brotherhood, 11 August 1929 in *Brothers Unite*, p. 37. There was a hope that another Bruderhof member might accompany Arnold, but that did not happen.

[101] Eberhard Arnold to David Wipf, 31 December 1929, in *Brothers Unite*, pp. 46-8.

believed in 'the goodness of man' and formed community on that basis.[102] Here was a reiteration of evangelical spirituality. Bender replied that he hoped those at the Rhön would be 'shining witnesses' of God's love and strength. He had found this personally: 'That is what you have become for me.'[103] Bender's developing thinking about the 'Anabaptist Vision' was to prove crucial for Mennonite self-identity. His ideas were published in *Church History* and in *The Mennonite Quarterly Review*, launched in 1927.[104] After Arnold arrived in America he reported home - in June 1930 - that he had attended a Mennonite meeting lasting many hours which had been 'astonishingly lively', with 'English revivalist songs'. Arnold had been able to speak for an hour, emphasising 'our special themes' - 'Pentecost at Jerusalem', 'the gospel of Christ', and 'love and community, in which everything belongs to God and to the church of the Spirit'.[105]

The journey to union with the Hutterites involved Arnold in visiting all thirty-three Hutterite communities. He spoke to each about unity and about funds for work in Germany. Arnold was questioned in detail at each stage of his journey about his communal Anabaptist credentials. Arnold's belief was that the Hutterites affirmed what was important, 'the gospel of personal conversion through the reconciling blood of Christ' and also 'the gospel applied to social relationships', putting into practice the Sermon on the Mount.[106] At the same time he found Hutterite communalism 'so totally supreme' that it seemed (as Arnold wrote in his diary) 'the salvation of the individual (also as regards eternal life) is seen solely in terms in terms of obedient yielding and surrender to the community'.[107] Arnold was concerned about lack of unity among the Hutterian communities, about economic disparity, and about Hutterite sermons drawing from seventeenth-century Hutterite life, rather than the vibrant early years of the

---

[102] Eberhard Arnold to Harold Bender, 20 May 1930, in *Brothers Unite*, p. 53.

[103] Harold Bender to Eberhard Arnold, 26 May 1930, in *Brothers Unite*, p. 54

[104] *Gospel Herald*, April 1994, p. 8.

[105] Eberhard Arnold to the Bruderhof community, 18 June 1930, in *Brothers Unite*, p. 64.

[106] Eberhard Arnold to John Horsch, 14 September to 9 October 1929, in *Brothers Unite*, p. 42.

[107] Eberhard Arnold, Diary, 21 July 1930, in *Brothers Unite*, p. 91.

movement.[108] The Hutterites, for their part, accepted Arnold on the basis of his biblical knowledge, study of Hutterite history, and commitment to community. Arnold was baptised and ordained 'in the service of the Word of God' with laying on of hands'.[109] Arnold was hesitant about having a further baptism as an adult. However, despite his reservations, he followed the Hutterite requirements.[110] There was excitement at the Rhön Bruderhof about the formal connection they now had with the Hutterite communities. Annemarie Wächter, a young teacher who joined the community, gave her family an idealistic account of the Hutterites: 'The inner life of their communities is still as pure, living and original as it was at the time of their formation.'[111]

Union with the Hutterites was to break down, be re-established and then cease again. Nonetheless, *Foundations* sees the early Hutterite movement as a defining influence on the Bruderhof, coupled with Johann Christoph Blumhardt (1805–1880) and his son Christoph Friedrich (Lutheran pastors who stressed Jesus as victor), and also the Youth Movements. *Foundations* outlines the Anabaptist movement's beginning, when 'Felix Manz, Conrad Grebel, and Georg Blaurock set the Radical Reformation in motion by accepting believer's baptism'. They 'championed freedom of conscience and a return to original Christianity in obedience to Jesus' words in the Gospels, rejecting armed force, infant baptism, and the institutional churches'.[112] *Foundations* notes the Hutterite model of communal living, although as Arnold Snyder observes, for Anabaptists more broadly – for Swiss Brethren (Manz, Grebel and Blaurock) and followers of Menno

---

[108] Janzen, 'The Hutterites and the Bruderhof', p. 6.

[109] Announcement, 20 March 1931, in *Brothers Unite*, p. 185.

[110] Janzen, 'The Hutterites and the Bruderhof', endnote 27, citing Michael Barnett, 'The Bruderhof (Society of Brothers) and the Hutterites in Historical Context', doctoral dissertation (Southwestern Baptist Theological Seminary, 1995), p. 103. See more below.

[111] *Anni: Letters and Writings of Annemarie* Wächter (Rifton, NY, and Robertsbridge: Plough Publishing House, 2010), p. 145. Letter from Annemarie of 28 February 1932 to Mama, Hilde and Reinhold. Annemarie later married Heinrich Arnold.

[112] *Foundations*, p. 25.

Simons - sharing of goods was a sign of the Body of Christ.[113]
Foundations explains that Hutterites shared 'money and possessions,
work, housing, and a common daily life', and zealously spread the
gospel, with hundreds suffering martyrdom. Issues that separated the
Bruderhof from the Hutterites are not discussed in *Foundations*. What
is affirmed is that the Bruderhof seeks to live 'in the same spirit as the
original Hutterites during the time of their first love and active
mission', and treasures Hutterian 'spiritual writings' - Hutter,
Riedemann, Ulrich Stadler, and Walpot.[114] The continuing influence
of the Youth Movements is noted in *Foundations*. For Arnold it was
very important, as he put it in 1935, to be 'simple', 'genuine', 'to have
nothing to do with anything forced, unnatural or artificial', including
'artificial piety'. The community 'wanted to live close to creation and
nature'. [115] The 'emphasis on simplicity and respect for creation' is,
Foundations states, 'essential to our community today', and, linked
with this, Bruderhof meetings are simple in form. Outdoor meetings
take place, in which 'the beauty of nature lifts our hearts and reminds
us of the greatness of our creator'.[116]

For the Bruderhof, as *Foundations* expresses it, any attempt to
force the practice of community produces only a disappointing
caricature. 'Church community is a gift of the Holy Spirit.' The
emphasis in *Foundations* is on God's help. Without that 'we human
beings are selfish and divided, unfit for life together'. The words of
Jesus are quoted, 'Apart from me you can do nothing.' The starting
point here is unequivocal: 'We remain sinners utterly dependent on
grace.'[117] At the same time, there are examples to follow. Hutterite
tradition has offered particular inspiration, but ultimately *Foundations*
points back to 'the first church founded at Pentecost in Jerusalem'.
Foundations argues that in this community 'the Spirit worked with
unique power, leading Christians to share all they had, to serve the
city's poor, and to proclaim the gospel boldly' and that 'this first
church community's life and teaching demonstrate what God's will is

---

[113] C. Arnold Snyder, *Following in the Footsteps of Christ* (London: Darton,
Longman and Todd, 2004), p. 145.

[114] *Foundations*, pp. 25-26.

[115] Arnold, *God's Revolution*, p. 147.

[116] *Foundations*, pp. 28, 65.

[117] *Foundations*, pp. 7-8.

for humankind'.[118] Whereas it has not been common among evangelicals to identify themselves with developments in Christian history following the death of the apostles, *Foundations* affirms 'the early church's rule of faith' and values 'the *Didache* and the writings of church fathers such as Clement of Rome, Hermas, Ignatius, Justin, Tertullian, and Origen'.[119] Not surprisingly, there is a focus in *Foundations* on movements that were communal: the Desert Fathers, the community around Augustine of Hippo, Celtic Christians, Waldensians, the Beguines and Beghards, followers of Francis of Assisi and Clare, Anabaptists and early Quakers, and the Moravians.[120] Bruderhof spirituality belongs to the communal and monastic traditions.

'The decisive outpouring of the Holy Spirit'

In the shaping of early Bruderhof spirituality, an understanding of the Holy Spirit was crucial. In one of Eberhard's first letters to Emmy, in April 1907, he spoke of revival he had heard about in Frederiksand, near Oslo, Norway, 'in which many came to a complete surrender to Jesus, and the Spirit descended with a power like that at Pentecost in the story in Acts, so that people are speaking in tongues there even today.'[121] This was a period of powerful spiritual movements in Europe. The Welsh Revival was described by F.B. Meyer as 'days of Pentecostal overflowing'.[122] A Methodist, T.B. Barratt, brought Pentecostalism to Norway. Support for Barratt came from Lewi Pethrus, a Swedish Baptist evangelist.[123] In 1907 Emmy heard four

---

[118] *Foundations*, p. 23.

[119] *Foundations*, pp. 23-4.

[120] *Foundations*, p. 24. Others individuals mentioned include John Wycliffe, Jan Hus, Martin Luther, Bach, Handel, John Wesley, Charles Finney, Hudson Taylor, Sadhu Sundar Singh, William and Catherine Booth, Fydor Dostoevsky, Dorothy Day, Mother Teresa, Sophie and Hans Scholl, Dietrich Bonhoeffer, Martin Luther King, Jr., and Oscar Romero.

[121] Baum, *Against the Wind*, p. 42.

[122] Frank Bartleman, *How Pentecost came to Los Angeles: As it was in the beginning* (Los Angeles: the author, 1925), p. 11; *The Christian*, 26 March 1925, p. 5.

[123] I.M. Randall, '"Days of Pentecostal Overflowing": Baptists and the shaping of Pentecostalism', in D.W. Bebbington, ed., *The Gospel in the World* (Carlisle:

Swedes who had came to Halle with the Pentecostal message. The Swedes told a Baptist meeting that they had been urged by the Holy Spirit to come to Halle even though they did not know there was such a town. Emmy, in discussion with them, was concerned that the cross of Christ was not central to their message.[124] Although Eberhard and Emmy did not identify with Pentecostalism, their desire was to follow what they felt was God's leading. On 27 April 1907 Emmy asked Eberhard about 'a question in regard to the Holy Spirit which worries me somewhat. I can't say that I've experienced a moment when I received the Holy Spirit, as for example [Charles] Finney or Fräulein von Nostiz can, to the degree that (like them) I could not control myself for joy.'[125] Eberhard acknowledged that Finney, the nineteenth-century evangelist, and von Nostiz, a leader in what Eberhard called the 'powerful awakening in Halle', and many others, 'received the Holy Spirit in a way that involved powerfully stirred emotions and other outward signs'. But, he considered, this 'must not make us think that the Spirit is limited to such accompanying phenomena... No one can call Jesus "Lord" (and thus belong to him) except through the Holy Spirit, as it says in 1 Corinthians 12:3.'[126]

This conjoining of Christ and the Spirit was something to which Eberhard Arnold would return again and again. At a conference of the SCM at Pentecost 1919, held on the Frauenberg, near Marburg, he spoke on the Sermon on the Mount. One report from a conference member spoke of how Arnold took the Sermon and 'burned it into our hearts with a passionate spirituality... Here there was no compromise... To be a Christian means to live the life of Christ.'[127] Arnold had published some of his thinking a few months before, in an article for the SCM. He argued against seeing the Sermon as a set of moralistic instructions and instead proposed that the way 'to attain the new life of the Sermon on the Mount' was through experiences that Paul spoke of as the 'liberation' of the believer from old ways and reception by believers of the 'life-giving spirit' of Jesus. 'In

---

Paternoster Press, 2002), pp. 80-104; N. Bloch-Hoell, *The Pentecostal Movement* (London: Allen & Unwin, 1964), pp. 66-72, 75-77.

[124] Emmy to Eberhard, 9 August 1907, BHA.

[125] Emmy to Eberhard, 27 April 1907, *Love Letters*, p. 39.

[126] Eberhard to Emmy, 28 April 1907, *Love Letters*, p. 43.

[127] Emmy Arnold, *Joyful Pilgrimage*, pp. 27-28.

fellowship with him [Jesus] we become the salt which overcomes the decay of death'.[128] This vision was reflected in responses to the conference. One SCM member spoke of 'the spirit of the Sermon on the Mount, the spirit of Jesus himself' taking hold of those present. 'We felt in Arnold's words that Jesus was seeking for our souls, seeking for us to belong to him completely, for us to love in earnest – and we strove for this with all our might.'[129]

The language of 'souls' might imply more concern with the Holy Spirit's work in inner spiritual life than with its outworking in human relationships. However, Arnold's view of spirituality was determinedly holistic. This is seen throughout his major work, *Innerland*, to which he gave energy from World War I onwards.[130] It is true that early in *Innerland* he wrote that in the hard times in which people were living, 'nothing but a thorough and deep-going revival of our inner life, a great and full awakening to God and his all-determining rulership, can bring the gospel to the whole world – the joyful news that Christ alone matters'. However, the life which mattered was outward as well as inward. He argued that for the gospel to spread 'the life of a missionary church must be given: a life that is in keeping with the kingdom of God from its core to the last detail of its outer form'. He saw this 'form' not in institutional terms, but typically for him, in pneumatological terms, 'as peace, unity, and community and as love and joy in the Holy Spirit'.[131] Arnold underlined the Spirit's work creating unity, prayerfulness and fellowship. 'Through the decisive outpouring of the Holy Spirit, all believers became so much one heart and one soul that they proved the uniting of all their powers, not only in the word of the apostles and in prayer, but also in the breaking of bread and in community – in full community of goods too.'[132] He explicitly countered the separation of soul and body: the Holy Spirit brings wholeness. He wrote: 'When we speak of the life of the soul, we usually think only of the innermost part of a believing spirit. But we have to remember that the soul embraces the whole of life.... What the believer must do, therefore, is

---

[128] Published April 1919, reproduced in Eberhard Arnold, *Salt and Light*, p. 52,

[129] Baum, *Against the Wind*, pp. 101-2.

[130] Arnold, *Innerland*, p. 4 (Preface).

[131] Arnold, *Innerland*, p. 13.

[132] Arnold, *Innerland*, p. 58.

search his innermost being, because his life in Christ shall be hidden in God.' He can say, 'I live, yet now it is no longer I but Christ who lives in me.'[133]

Emmy Arnold noted the importance for the Bruderhof community, as it developed and grew, of the celebration of Pentecost, or Whitsun. She spoke of Whitsun as 'our feast'. It was following the Whitsun 1920 conference that the community was formed in Sannerz. This conference included a time on the top of a hill when a Whitsun fire was lit and it seemed as if the blaze, symbolising 'the burning up of the old and the coming of something new', was a means through which God was speaking. There was folk dancing and singing of songs. Dances were seen as spiritual experiences, as Eberhard Arnold wrote in one of his poems:

> Spirit-gripped, / Move as one.
> Circle round, / Centre-bound!

An English Quaker who was present at the conference, recommended from Quaker tradition a time of silence 'to listen to the Spirit'.[134] In *Innerland*, Arnold drew out this emphasis on listening to the Spirit in Hutterite tradition. He quoted Riedemann: 'Just as in speaking we exhale and let our breath out with words so that a living breath of wind blows from both the speaker and the spoken word and a voice comes out and makes a sound, so the Holy Spirit comes from the Father and the Son or from the truth and the word.' Riedemann used the picture of fire, heat, and light for the Trinity: 'if we lack one of them, we lack them all; for just as little as heat and light can be taken away from fire and yet leave it a fire, just so little and even less can the Son and the Holy Spirit be taken away from the Father.' Arnold was fascinated by the idea of renewal continually witnessing to relational reality in God.[135]

In one of his last addresses, shortly before his death, Arnold spoke of the first Anabaptists as 'a community of heart and life based on the Spirit' and he contrasted this with the Reformed view of 'the church

---

[133] Arnold, *Innerland*, p. 85.

[134] Emmy Arnold, *Joyful Pilgrimage*, pp. 34-5, 5.

[135] Arnold, *Innerland*, p. 311

as a state-constituted society based on law'.[136] The life of
contemporary Hutterite communities in America with which the
Bruderhof were now in fellowship, however, seemed to involve
numerous laws. Emmy Arnold wrote of Hutterite customs: head
covering for women; black and dark grey clothes for men, instead of
the bright colours of the German youth movement; or the rejection of
the musical instruments that added so much to folk singing.[137]
Although these Hutterite practices were accepted by the Bruderhof at
the time, Eberhard Arnold wrote: 'There is no other church of Jesus
Christ than the one completely free of human authority, built and
directed by the spirit of Christ's sacrifice. She remains at one in the
Holy Spirit, the one foundation of truth, the very soul of readiness for
the cross.'[138] The imposition of 'human authority' was at odds with
Arnold's own spirit. By stressing unity in the Spirit, Arnold did not
mean to promote uniformity. The opposite was the case. He wrote:
'We have never found it disturbing when people have come to us
representing convictions that differ from ours... Each one will bring
from the storehouse of his earlier convictions those elements that are
true, and he will find these again.' Arnold was not impressed by any
unity that was produced 'by forcing anyone to comply'.[139]

It seems that the way in which Arnold understood the 'outpouring
of the Holy Spirit' had more in common with dynamic forms of
evangelical spirituality than with the way Hutterite tradition had
developed. Thus Arnold spoke of the 'key to the Bible' as 'Christ and
his Holy Spirit' and added that anyone who relies on the 'letter' of
Scripture 'stands before firmly locked gates'.[140] As Arnold put it in
May 1934 (speaking on 'we must hold to Jesus'), Christ who 'truly
rose from the dead' is 'the Risen One' and is 'present in the church
through the pouring out of the Holy Spirit', in 'fulfilment of his
promise' in Matthew 28.[141] Tyldesley suggests that 'it should be noted

---

[136] Eberhard Arnold, *The Early Anabaptists* (Rifton, NY, and Robertsbridge:
Plough Publishing House, 1970), p. 27.

[137] Emmy Arnold, *Joyful Pilgrimage*, p. 113.

[138] Arnold, *Innerland*, p. 33.

[139] Arnold, *God's Revolution*, pp. 38-9

[140] Arnold, *Innerland*, p. 373.

[141] Eberhard Arnold, Sermon preached on 13 May 1934, published in *Plough
Quarterly* (Summer 2014), p. 18 (see pages 10-19).

that prior to the turn towards life in Christian community, Arnold had been an Evangelical Christian'.[142] This implies that after his 'turn towards life in Christian community' Arnold was no longer an evangelical Christian, but in July 1934 Arnold affirmed that it was 'truly Christian' to 'proclaim the good news of the pardoned sinner, who is now able to lead a purified life'. Arnold quoted Colossians 1:18 and added that the New Testament, indeed the whole Bible, spoke of this experience. He expressed thankfulness for many movements that had witnessed to Jesus as Saviour. 'Such waves of inner revival keep recurring, and that is a great grace.'[143] To balance this, however, while there was joy when people knew 'forgiveness of sins in his [Jesus'] death on the cross', as Arnold stated in November 1934, 'Christ's love and the meaning of his death on the cross are not fully understood if they are restricted to the individual's subjective experience of salvation.'[144] In July 1935 Arnold linked this with the Spirit's presence 'in the so-called outward aspects of life just as much as in the innermost concerns of faith'.[145]

Perhaps the connection between Eberhard Arnold's evangelical spirituality and his vision for a community living in the power of the Holy Spirit was most fully expressed in a substantial letter Arnold wrote to his sister, Hannah, in March 1925. Hannah was involved, as Eberhard had been, in the Fellowship movement, and Eberhard affirmed that 'building up the Fellowship and evangelizing have always been an essential part of my life, the life given me by God'. He was adamant in his letter that it was 'a totally false report, if you have been told that I ever expressed myself about the Fellowship or Revival Movement or its Christianity in such a way as to reject it'. Arnold insisted that 'it is impossible to emphasize the forgiveness of sins too strongly'. What Arnold did oppose was 'when in spite of the experience of forgiveness a person looks away from this great heart of God and gets enmeshed in his own small heart, becoming completely lost in his personal experience'. He wrote later in the letter:

---

[142] Tyldesley, *No Heavenly Delusion?*, p. 76.

[143] Arnold, *God's Revolution*, July 1934, p. 43.

[144] Arnold, *God's Revolution*, November 1934, p. 42.

[145] Arnold, *God's Revolution*, July 1935, p. 43.

We all love the third chapter of John's Gospel, but we tend to forget that personal rebirth is here placed in the supra-personal context of the kingdom of God. The coming kingdom is the determining element in the Bible. It is this kingdom of the future that must overwhelm and completely fill us. The Holy Spirit wants to come over us and fill us in order to lead us into the future kingdom; the Spirit is to bring to life for us Jesus' words about the world of the future; the Spirit is to lead us toward this, so that we become a living example, a parable, a visible testimony of the coming kingdom.[146]

In Arnold's mind, the Bruderhof was one such 'visible testimony'.

A paragraph in *Foundations* echoes Arnold's thinking about the 'Holy Spirit who wants to come over us and fill us':

As described in Acts 2 and 4, the Holy Spirit descended on the believers who had gathered after Jesus' resurrection, and the first communal church was born. Just as it was then, so it will be today whenever the Spirit is poured out on a group of people. They will be filled with love for Christ and for one another, and their communion of love will lead them to share their goods, talents, and lives, boldly testifying to the gospel. This is our calling in church community.[147]

There is realism in *Foundations* about the Bruderhof as a movement that will pass away, but also confidence that 'the stream of life to which it belongs can never pass away'. Remaining part of the stream of God's Spirit is seen as 'possible through an ever new encounter with Christ.'[148] Because of the desire for 'daily life together to be inspired and led by the Holy Spirit', attention is given to establishing church order 'based on Scripture and the example of the early church and shaped by the Anabaptist tradition and our own experience'. This is balanced by the conviction that no system of church order should hold back the leading of 'the spirit of Christ', since he is 'the head of

---

[146] Eberhard Arnold to Hannah Arnold, March 1925. This hitherto unpublished letter is held in the Bruderhof archive, File BHA, EA 25/15. See Appendix 1.

[147] *Foundations*, p. 7.

[148] *Foundations*, p. 28.

the church, and he supersedes all human authorities and traditions'.[149]
There is also an emphasis on prayer, which *Foundations* describes as
'the lifeblood of church community' and which takes many forms –
silent, communal, fasting and singing.[150]

As in the thinking of Eberhard Arnold, *Foundations* reflects on
unity and diversity in the Christian community. Quoting 1 Corinthians
12:4-7, 'there are varieties of gifts, but the same Spirit; and there are
varieties of service, but the same Lord; and there are varieties of
working, but it is the same God who inspires them all in every one',
Foundations notes that some members of the fellowship 'receive the
gift to teach, some to counsel and encourage, some to proclaim the
gospel, some to praise God through music and art, some to care for the
needy, some to contribute in other practical ways. But the greatest gift,
offered to each of us, is the ability to love'.[151] In terms of decisions in
the community, Arnold looked for unanimity, which he saw as 'the
opposite of making a majority decision'.[152] Similarly, *Foundations*
speaks of decisions being 'the expression of a unanimity freely arrived
at through common discernment and prayers', which 'comes from
listening together to God's Spirit'. Thus 'decision-making by
democratic or congregational vote' is rejected, and the 'rule of human
opinions, whether of the majority or the minority', is described as 'the
enemy of the rule of the Holy Spirit'. However, *Foundations*
encourages members to speak their minds: 'Unanimity in the Spirit is
not conformity. It cannot be manufactured through consensus-
building, persuasion, or pressure. In our experience, the dissent of a
single voice has at times proved to be prophetic.'[153] A spirituality that
involved a sense of being empowered by the Spirit to engage in
prophetic witness had brought the Bruderhof into being.

Spirituality in the church: 'a sacrament, a living symbol'

On 13 September 1907 Eberhard Arnold wrote to Emmy to say that he
was going to 'withdraw from the established church, since I consider

---

[149] *Foundations*, p. 29
[150] *Foundations*, p. 65.
[151] *Foundations*, pp. 39-40
[152] Arnold, *God's Revolution*, Arnold in1929, p. 39.
[153] *Foundations*, pp. 45-6.

it dishonest through and through and contrary to the spirit of the Bible; and that his desire was to embrace as his ideal 'church communities who use church discipline and celebrate the Lord's Supper'.[154] As well as indicating the strength of Arnold's biblical convictions, this also shows that in the midst of his experience of revival he had a sense of the importance of the church. Thus Tyldesley does not grasp the essence of Arnold when he talks about 'a collision between the individualism of the revival movement and the communal aspects of the Youth Movement' and suggests that Arnold's thinking moved towards the youth movement.[155] Rather, speaking to the Rhön Bruderhof in November 1928 Arnold accorded 'the earliest Baptizers' the primary influence on the Bruderhof, and considered that the Fellowship movements of the earlier twentieth century had 'lost power', as did other movements, 'such as German Christian Students'. Arnold talked about the Youth and workers' communal movements as having 'some elements that were genuine', but this was mixed with other elements and they 'grew weaker and weaker in their real effectiveness'.[156] He was looking for renewal of spiritual experience.

The radical views about the established churches that Arnold voiced in 1907 could still be heard in his later writings. In *Innerland* he wrote about the 'pentecostal spring' of Christian beginnings contrasting sharply with 'the icy rigidity of our Christianity today'. In the Early Church, he argued, 'a fresher wind blew and purer water flowed, a stronger power and a more fiery warmth ruled than today among all those who call themselves Christians'. Arnold believed it was accepted that 'the community life of faith and love represented by the early church is almost not to be found today'.[157] This seems to indicate a low estimation of those seeking to witness to Christ in his time. However, a few pages further on in *Innerland* Arnold struck a more hopeful note: 'In the authority of the Holy Spirit, the whole church is of one heart and one mind... Her unfeigned love and boundless faith long to put everything to the service of God. She wants to summon all the nations of the world to partake in God's

---

[154] Eberhard to Emmy, 13 September 1907, *Love Letters*, p. 145.

[155] Tyldesley, *No Heavenly Delusion?*, p. 80.

[156] Eberhard Arnold, November 1928, in *Brothers Unite*, p. 11.

[157] Arnold, *Innerland*, p. 315.

kingdom.'[158] Exactly how the features of 'icy rigidity' and 'unfeigned love' can be reconciled is not clear. The vision of the unity of the whole church is then expounded in this remarkable statement: 'Like Mary the virgin, the church is, through the Holy Spirit, the eternal mother. Without her there are no children... The church takes shape only where the Holy Spirit has brought about a life and faith completely at one with the whole glorified band of martyrs and witnesses, with the apostolic mother church of all centuries.'[159] Here is a high view of the church, one that coheres with a catholic ecclesiology.

In similar vein, Arnold wrote to his sister Hannah in 1925 about how in the Reformation period 'many were really in unity in the eyes of God and in the eyes of faith - the Lutherans and the Zwinglians, believing Catholics like Staupitz for example, the biblicist Schwenkfeldian movement of the Holy Spirit, the communistic peace churches of the Baptizers, and many other shadings of the Reformation era'. Arnold's vision was of 'the fulfilment of Jesus' plea' - 'that they may all be one'. By this unity, the world will 'recognize that Jesus was sent by God.'[160] In practice, however, unity was hard to achieve. In 1930 a couple who were later important in the Bruderhof, Hans and Margrit Meier, joined with others to start a communal settlement in Längimoos: the *Werkhof* (Work Farm). But by 1932, with the *Werkhof* deeply divided, some members looked to the Bruderhof.[161] The *Werkhof* was inspired by Leonard Ragaz, whose communal-orientated thinking had been shaped by Hermann Kutter. Shared admiration for Kutter meant Ragaz and Arnold corresponded in the 1920s, but Ragaz felt his work was being criticised by Arnold. Ragaz asked if the Bruderhof considered their community '*a* church or

---

[158] Arnold, *Innerland*, p. 322.

[159] Arnold, *Innerland*, p. 332.

[160] Eberhard Arnold to Hannah Arnold, March 1925: BHA, EA 25/15.

[161] Hans Meier, 'As Long as there is Light' [1995], is an unpublished autobiography. See also Dejan Adam, '"The Practical, Visible Witness of Discipleship": The Life and Convictions of Hans Meier (1902-1992)', in K.G. Jones and I.M. Randall, eds.,*Counter-Cultural Communities: Baptistic Life in Twentieth-Century Europe* (Milton Keynes: Paternoster, 2008), pp. 285-335.

the church – excluding other forms of the church'.[162] Arnold's reply has become recognised as a classic statement and is echoed in *Foundations*.[163] He began: 'It is of decisive importance that we remember the mission of the church as it is laid upon us in the outpouring of the Holy Spirit.'[164] Arnold explained that as 'weak and needy people' the Bruderhof community was not 'the' church, rather 'the recipients of God's love – people 'unworthy and unfit for the work of the Holy Spirit, for the building of the church, and for its mission to the world'. Then he stated: 'But if anyone asks, "Does the church of God come down to you?" then we have to answer yes... The church is wherever the Holy Spirit is.'[165]

The emphasis on the Spirit did not mean that Arnold neglected the sacraments. On baptism, he wrote in June 1907 to Emmy that he could no longer find 'compelling proof *for* infant baptism' in the church's life. When reading scripture and praying he felt he had quenched 'the light of understanding' with regard to baptism – 'even if without wanting to'.[166] Writing again to Emmy later in June he wanted to reach a 'calm, clearly reasoned conviction'. If he was suddenly baptised people would say, 'First the Salvation Army and now baptism. He's always going to extremes! It's because of his temperament!'[167] By September 1907 he wished to be baptised as soon as possible and leave the established church.[168] Emmy replied: 'I still don't have a definite position on baptism, though one thing I do know is that I personally didn't get *anything* out of my being baptized as a baby. I don't feel the slightest blessing in it. I came to God through my conversion, not through baptism.'[169] Eberhard began to baptise others from 1920 onwards. In his 1925 summary of 'Why We

---

[162] Leonhard Ragaz to the Bruderhof, 22 February 1933, cited by Barth, *An Embassy Besieged*, p. 40.

[163] *Foundations*, p. 9

[164] *Eberhard Arnold: Modern Spiritual Masters Series* (Maryknoll, NY: Orbis Books, 2000), p. 133. Emmy Barth quotes Arnold's reply to Ragaz but has not included this part of the quotation.

[165] *Eberhard Arnold: Modern Spiritual Masters*, pp. 133-4.

[166] Eberhard to Emmy, 16 June 1907, *Love Letters*, pp. 91-2.

[167] Eberhard to Emmy, 29-30 June 1907, *Love Letters*, p. 103.

[168] Eberhard to Emmy, 4 September 1907, *Love Letters*, p. 133.

[169] Emmy to Eberhard, 25 June 1907, *Love Letters*, p. 94.

Live in Community' Arnold spoke of 'baptism by immersion' as signifying purification, death to an evil life, and resurrection.[170] His own baptism and his practice of baptism meant that Arnold found it problematic when in 1930 he had to be baptised into the Hutterites. He explained to them that he could not deny his earlier baptism by immersion with its 'sense of incorporation into the body of Christ'. He found it (as he noted in his diary) 'quite hard to submit to the baptism of pouring over', but he saw it as incorporation into the Hutterite Brotherhood and he was helped by reading about some three-fold baptisms in the early church.[171]

From September 1920 the Lord's Supper (the term used) was celebrated at Sannerz. Guests who testified to being disciples of Jesus could take part in the Supper.[172] In 'Why We Live in Community', Arnold spoke of the Lord's Supper or 'Meal of Remembrance' as a witness to Christ's death and his second coming and an occasion when 'we receive him in ourselves'.[173] The 'receiving' added to 'remembrance' suggests an understanding of the Supper as a spiritual experience. It was also a time for the community to reflect together. In thinking about the Supper the Bruderhof drew from older traditions of the church, such as the *Didache*, with its reference to the fruit of the earth in bread and wine.[174] In January 1933 Arnold spoke of the Bruderhof practice at the Supper. The aim was to 'combine simplicity with real joy in God's gifts to us'. There was no sense of one person being in charge. The practice was similar to that in Anabaptist and Baptist communities. Arnold wrote: 'According to the age-old custom of simple folk, the loaf is passed around, and each person breaks off a piece and passes it on to the next.' There was a similar procedure with the wine jug. For Arnold this passing around was important. There could 'hardly be a more powerful expression of community'.[175] A few months later Arnold stressed diversity in this unity: 'the more varied

---

[170] Arnold, *Why We Live in Community*, pp. 16-17.

[171] Eberhard Arnold, Diary entries from 1 December 1930, in *Brothers Unite*, pp. 181-2.

[172] Baum, *Against the Wind*, p. 130.

[173] Arnold, *Why We Live in Community*, pp. 16-17.

[174] Arnold, *God's Revolution*, May 1934, pp. 71-3.

[175] Arnold, *God's Revolution*, January 1933, pp. 73-4.

our different backgrounds are, the richer the fruits of this diversity will be'.[176]

The songs sung at Sannerz similarly conveyed this diversity. Vollmer goes so far as to suggest that the songs which were collected in the early Sannerz song-book 'manifest most clearly the spiritual productivity of the circle'. She notes that included in the songbook were folk songs, hymns from the Reformation and the Anabaptists, songs of the Moravian Brethren and the revival movements, songs of the youth movement and the workers' movement, and many poems by Eberhard Arnold and Otto Salomon, who was from a Jewish family. Salomon embraced Christianity and worked as a literary and artistic director. He was at Sannerz for two years.[177] Where folk songs that were appreciated at Sannerz did not convey a Christian message, Sannerz members felt free to make changes. The best known was the addition of a fourth stanza to the well-known *Kein schöner Land* ('Earth has no fairer countryside'), by Eva Oehlke, an early Sannerz member, to make it Christocentric:

> Brothers, you know what makes us one:
> For us shines bright another Sun.
> In Him we're living,
> For Him we're striving,
> The Church at one![178]

The singing developed at Sannerz drew from varied sources, creatively incorporating old traditions and new expressions of spirituality – diversity in unity.

The sense of being united with the whole church throughout the centuries and throughout the world in all its diversity is pervasive in *Foundations*. In the first section 'the apostolic rule of faith in the triune God as stated in the Apostles' and Nicene Creeds' is affirmed.[179] Thomas Finger suggests that it is hard to find in the rest of *Foundations* anything specific from these creeds, except that they

---

[176] Arnold, *God's Revolution*, pp. 38-9

[177] Vollmer, 'The *Neuwerk* Movement', p. 75; cf. p. 61, fn. 47, for Salomon, who was to be involved in publishing and ecumenical work in Germany and Switzerland.

[178] Vollmer, 'The *Neuwerk* Movement', p. 76.

[179] *Foundations*, p. 1.

are confessed at baptism.[180] Although this is true, the emphasis on continuity with tradition, in worship and witness, is evident. Thus *Foundations* states: 'Our church community is only a small part of the universal church. This universal church is the body of Christ, made up of all who belong to him; it is his bride, set apart for him alone. It cannot be identified with any human institution or group... it includes the apostles, prophets, martyrs, and believers from every age who are with God as the "cloud of witnesses" from every nation, tribe, and race.'[181] There is explicit continuity with monastic traditions, in vows that members make of poverty - 'We pledge to give up all property and to live simply, in complete freedom from possessions' - chastity - 'We pledge to uphold sexual purity and, if married, to stay faithful in the bond of marriage between one man and one woman for life' - and obedience, 'to Christ and our brothers and sisters.' These are accompanied by promises by the new member, focused on loyalty to Christ and the community. There is laying on of hands and prayer 'that God will fill him or her anew with the Holy Spirit'.[182]

Foundations speaks of life in church community as 'a sacrament, a living symbol that illustrates God's calling for humankind'. There is a desire to embrace variety, 'as the Spirit leads', while maintaining 'our common faith in one baptism, one calling, one profession of vows, and one Spirit of love who guides us in all things'.[183] In my visits to the Darvell Bruderhof community in the south of England I have been able to speak to a number of members of the community about their spiritual lives. Those I have talked to are at different stages of life, from twenties to sixties, and are involved in different roles in the community. There was clear evidence of variety and affirmation of the fact that people have different experiences. At the same time there was a striking amount of common ground in relation to the guidance of God in individual lives. The stories that were told spoke of 'personal faith in Jesus', experience of Jesus that 'changed my life', 'prayer as a life line', a 'journey to a deeper inner life', 'openness to the leading of the Holy Spirit', seeking to be 'biblical' and to read the Bible, feeling 'free' in the decision to be baptised, 'finding joy', knowing 'open

---

[180] Finger, 'Review', p. 586.

[181] *Foundations*, p. 9.

[182] *Foundations*, pp. 34-5.

[183] *Foundations*, p. 63.

sharing' in the community and being 'led in a certain direction', 'unity of heart and peace over issues', embracing the 'Great Commission' to spread the 'good news', 'being willing to go', 'working in this world', not 'living for self' but 'serving', and community as 'a wonderful gift but not an end in itself'.[184] In the fellowship, says *Foundations* in a section on the individual in community, 'we will find diverse reflections of God's image'.[185]

Baptism and the Lord's Supper are covered in a major section in *Foundations*, 'Church Actions', which also includes laying on of hands, church discipline and forgiveness, and marriage. Baptism is offered to anyone 'who believes in the gospel of Jesus Christ and whose repentance comes from the heart, bearing fruit in deeds'. There is a desire to be open to spiritual experience in baptism. The one conducting the baptism 'will lay his hands on the newly baptized and pray that Jesus will fill them with "power from on high" – with the Holy Spirit'.[186] The Lord's Supper is seen as 'a meal of communion with Christ', and reference is made to Jesus' words, 'This is my body... This is my blood', and: 'He who eats my flesh and drinks my blood abides in me, and I in him.' There are indications of a sacramental understanding of the actions of a united body of believers ruled by the Spirit. Thus *Foundations* continues: 'By partaking of the bread and wine, we renew our covenant of baptism, giving ourselves to Jesus in full surrender and declaring our readiness to suffer and die for him. We believe that he himself will be present among us with his power to heal the sick, forgive sins, and drive out evil.'[187] Perhaps this echoes the influence on Arnold of the Blumhardts, who saw Jesus bringing healing and deliverance.[188] It is not entirely clear from *Foundations* who is able to come to the Lord's Table. Seeking to follow the Early Church, the Bruderhof 'celebrate the Lord's Supper only with those who have received believer's baptism, who affirm the

---

[184] I am most grateful to those who spoke to me about their experiences.

[185] *Foundations*, p. 76.

[186] *Foundations*, p. 50.

[187] *Foundations*, p. 53.

[188] Baum, *Against the Wind*, pp. 146-8. On Johann Christoph Blumhardt, see Friedrich Zuendel, *The Awakening: One Man's Battle with Darkness* (Rifton, NY, and Robertsbridge: Plough Publishing House, 2000).

same confession of faith, and with whom there is peace and unity'.[189] Finger takes this as a 'strict limitation to tiny groups',[190] and if this means the Supper is open only to Bruderhof members it is restrictive, in view of the many believers who would affirm 'peace and unity' with the Bruderhof. If the 'confession of faith' is the Apostles' and Nicene Creeds, this of course opens up much wider possibilities for fellowship.

More attention is given to church discipline in *Foundations* than seems to have been the case within the early Bruderhof. However, church discipline is a recognition that the spiritual life of a community is not without problems. After the death of Eberhard Arnold, as Emmy recorded, the Bruderhof suffered from 'disloyalty and cowardice, gossip, cliquish friendships, self-pity, excessive sympathy for some, and insufficient compassion for others'.[191] In *Foundations* there is reference to Christ entrusting the church 'with the gift of church discipline, commissioning it to confront and overcome sin and to declare forgiveness in his name to the repentant.' This discipline is linked with being a disciple and with 'training and correction'.[192] The most common understanding of church discipline in the Anabaptist tradition is of an action taken by the church, and this aspect is present in *Foundations*, but the emphasis is on a different kind of church discipline – a gift 'granted only to those who desire and request it'. This is defined as 'a time of repentance', of 'silent reflection', and a time when 'the church community shows its special love to those in discipline, caring for their practical needs with special consideration and keeping them constantly in its prayers'. *Foundations* states categorically that such discipline 'is not a punishment and has nothing in common with shunning, expulsion, or any kind of coercion; to abuse it for any such purpose is a sin.' The intended outcome is deeper spiritual experience: 'assurance of a cleansed heart and God's peace'.[193]

---

[189] *Foundations*, p. 53

[190] Finger, 'Review', p. 589.

[191] Emmy Arnold, *Joyful Pilgrimage*, p. 154.

[192] *Foundations*, p. 55.

[193] *Foundations*, pp. 57-8.

'The Way of Peace'

This peace, however, for the Bruderhof, is never simply an inward peace, but a commitment to making a difference in a world which lacks peace. In *Foundations*, under the heading 'The Way of Peace', there is a picture of Christ calling his church 'to be the embassy of his kingdom of peace, stationed in the present age as in a foreign jurisdiction'. This calling can include 'working together with others of goodwill, whether or not they are confessing believers'.[194] It seems that this concept of the 'embassy' may have first been proposed in March 1933 by Annemarie Wächter at a Good Friday Bruderhof meeting. At this meeting the Lord's Supper was celebrated, and there was also discussion of the response of the community to the rise of the Nazi movement. A year before, Annemarie had written to her parents to try to explain the community's commitment to social justice.[195] At the March 1933 community meeting she said that listening to a speech Hitler had just delivered she 'felt as though we [in the Bruderhof] were an embassy in another country, with a completely different language and a completely different atmosphere'. She called on the community to give powerful testimony, to 'stand completely in the joy and power of the Spirit'.[196] As Nazi power grew, the witness of the Bruderhof marked them out and led to Gestapo raids, interrogation, harassment, imprisonment of three members in Fulda prison, and the ultimate dissolution of the Rhön community. As Baum notes, no member ever lifted a hand in the German salute or became a storm trooper.[197]

The Bruderhof movement became known for its outright opposition to war. *Foundations* states that Bruderhof members 'will not serve in the armed forces of any country, not even as non-combatants'.[198] This was not Eberhard Arnold's position prior to the First World War. In 1914, when war broke out in Europe, Arnold had a book, *Inward Life* (which eventually became *Innerland*), prepared

---

[194] *Foundations*, p. 11.
[195] *Anni*, p. 135. Letter of 6 February 1932 from Annemarie to Mama, Hilde and Reinhold.
[196] Barth, *An Embassy Besieged*, p. 44.
[197] Baum, *Against the Wind*, p. 221.
[198] *Foundations*, p. 12.

for press, but in view of the war he revised it, introducing patriotic themes and changing the title to *The War: A Call to Inwardness*. The way the cover was designed, and in part the contents, aligned it with books being produced to support Germany's 'just and righteous war'.[199] Arnold was willing to join a reserve unit in August 1914, but his health was not strong enough for military service. In 1915 he started work for the SCM, editing the magazine *Die Furche* (The Furrow), and developing the Furche Publishing House. SCM leaders were supportive of the war, but there is evidence in 1916 that Arnold's own thinking was changing. In the margin of a song sheet, 'Hymn of hate against England', Arnold wrote, 'Love?'[200] Before the end of 1917, Arnold began to revise his book. All nationalistic sections were removed. He restructured his work as a journey into the 'inner land of the unseen, to God and the Spirit' and as a 'guide into the soul of the Bible'.[201] In a speech he delivered in November 1917, Arnold called for a 'rebirth in our hearts' and an abandonment of 'the alien spirits of hatred and violence, of lying, impure and greedy possessiveness'.[202]

This renewed spiritual emphasis did not mean that Arnold drew back from involvement in society. The opposite is the case. At a conference in Tambach, in September 1919, Karl Barth spoke on the task of the church as not being to try to bring in the kingdom by human methods, since God alone was at work in the world. The task of the Christian, as Barth stated it, was to 'pay careful heed to what God is doing'.[203] Arnold offered a response. Although there were aspects of Barth's approach with which he agreed, Arnold considered that the influence of what he called 'modern theology', by which he meant Barthian thinking, had been 'disastrous'. Arnold was glad that there had been the stress - clearly seen in Barth - on God as 'totally other than all our movements for personal salvation or social reform'. But this one-sided emphasis, Arnold argued, 'is bound to have the effect of minimizing or even suppressing social responsibility'.[204] As Nazi power increased, Hans Meier, on behalf of the Bruderhof, met

---

[199] Baum, *Against the Wind*, pp. 80-1.

[200] Baum, *Against the Wind*, pp. 85-90.

[201] Baum, *Against the Wind*, p. 93.

[202] *Eberhard Arnold: Modern Spiritual Masters*, p. 32.

[203] Vollmer, 'The *Neuwerk* Movement', p. 21.

[204] Arnold, *God's Revolution*, p. 42.

the German Lutheran Pastor and key figure in the Confessing Church, Martin Niemöller.[205] Niemöller, Barth, Dietrich Bonhoeffer and others met in Barmen in May 1934 and produced the famous *Barmen Declaration*, condemning the cult of the Führer. Two years later it was apparent at a World Mennonite Conference in Amsterdam that no German Mennonite congregation was prepared to stand up against the Nazis with regard to military service, but at a small meeting eighteen Mennonite leaders, and Emmy Arnold and Hans Zumpe from the Bruderhof, signed a declaration calling for opposition to 'the sin of war' and committing themselves to the 'proclamation of the gospel of peace'.[206]

The main ways in which Arnold pursued the vision of achieving social change were through publishing, lecturing to a variety of groups across Germany, and the education of children and young people. He spoke of educational work 'as a work of worship'.[207] Arnold became director for two years of the Neuwerk Publishing House and was able to bring Quaker funding into his publishing project, specifically for the magazine *Das Neue Werk*. Alongside this magazine, the community in Sannerz became involved in the publication of *Die Wegwarte*, the magazine of German Baptist Youth. Wider links across Europe, as well as in Germany, were important. The Jewish philosopher Martin Buber helped with Neuwerk conferences. Arnold became involved in the international Fellowship of Reconciliation (FOR), a body which drew together pacifists from different traditions. Arnold was particularly supportive of the radical pacifism of Kees Boeke, in Holland.[208] In England Charles Raven, Regius Professor of Divinity in Cambridge, was one of the FOR's major spokesmen. He delivered an apologia in 1934, published as *Is War Obsolete?* (1935). Raven became chairman of the FOR, and in language that was in tune with Arnold, urged Christians to seek to convince others 'that the

---

[205] Barth, *An Embassy Besieged*, p. 124.

[206] Barth, *No Lasting Home*, pp. xiv, xv, 195-8. The leading figure was a Dutch Mennonite, Jacob ter Meulen, a friend of Eberhard Arnold. Hans Zumpe was married to Emi-Margret Arnold.

[207] Baum, *Against the Wind*, p. 177.

[208] Vollmer, 'The Neuwerk Movement', pp. 66-70.

power of the Spirit is stronger than the arms of the flesh and that in these days warfare is as obsolete and as intolerable as slavery'.[209]

In the mid-1920s Arnold tried to launch a massive publishing project, which was only partly successful. What he had in mind, as he put it, was 'a [multi-volume] series drawn from the living testimony of Christian witnesses across the centuries'. The title given to the series was *Quellen* – source books.[210] Arnold wanted to show the witness of the church through the centuries. Although his own sympathies were with the Anabaptists, he was happy to envisage publishing the work of Ignatius of Loyola, whose spirituality was of such significance. Arnold tried unsuccessfully to recruit Karl Barth as an advisor for his project. The first volume to appear was one on Zinzendorf. Volumes appeared between 1925 and 1926 on the early seventeenth-century mystical writer Jakob Böhme, on the Danish philosopher Søren Kierkegaard, and on Francis of Assisi.[211] Arnold found links between different movements in the history of the church. He noted that Francis of Assisi began each conversation or address he gave with 'Peace be with you', and that this was true of many Anabaptists. Arnold went on: 'So today too we must confront the unpeace of the whole world with the words of true brotherhood.' He wanted not only proclamation of peace but also a demonstration of that peace in lived experience.[212]

In December 1926, as part of his publishing project, Arnold produced his book, *The Early Christians after the Death of the Apostles*. This was an important work of scholarship, the result of the collection and translation of many documents by Arnold and by Else von Hollander. Arnold wrote a vivid commentary on these early Christian writings. For him the Early Church was the example *par excellence* of a counter-cultural community of peace. This peace was not passivity or a spirit of resignation to the dominance of evil. On the other hand, the early Christians did not seek to overcome evil through human power. Their power lay in their dedication to the way of Christ. Arnold wrote: 'To believers living in the time of the early church and

---

[209] C.E. Raven, *Is War Obsolete?* (London: Allen and Unwin, 1935), p. 183

[210] I am grateful to Margret Gneiting who showed me some first editions during a visit I made to Sannerz.

[211] Baum, *Against the Wind*, pp. 166-7.

[212] Arnold, *Innerland*, pp. 246-7.

of the Apostle Paul, the cross was the one and only proclamation. Christians knew only one way, that of being nailed to the Cross with Christ. Only dying his death with him, they felt, could possibly lead to resurrection and to the kingdom.'[213] Later he took up the theme of martyrdom. What Arnold wrote in 1926 can be seen as prophetic: 'The early Christians were revolutionaries of the Spirit... Their witness meant they had to reckon with being sentenced to death by state and society.... To give witness is the essence of martyrdom.'[214] A decade later, a period of seventeen years of Bruderhof community witness in Germany ended. Emmy Arnold spoke of 'the loss of everything we had' and added, 'one might well ask how it was possible for us to go on'. Her answer was: 'We had heard the call clearly, and there was no choice but to follow it.'[215]

It was in *Innerland*, in its final form, that Arnold set out most fully what he meant by the 'way of peace'. He argued that it was possible to speak of the 'militant peace of Jesus Christ' and contended that this was 'unknown to humankind'. What was found in the world was either 'hate with its murderous preparation for war' or else 'the insincere and uncreative flabbiness of peace without struggle and without unity'.[216] Nor did Arnold believe there was necessarily peace when nations abstained from war. For him social justice was essential. He wrote in typically trenchant terms: 'No peace and disarmament without social justice! No prophet recognizes peace and disarmament or the changing of deadly weapons into tools of civilization without social renewal and reconciliation, giving back to the poor the use of all tools and products.'[217] It was this message which Arnold believed was missing in many presentations of the gospel. But the true church witnessed not only to peace with God but also love to God and to others. 'When we are gathered in the church, and God's love fills our hearts', he wrote, 'we cannot be tempted by any power that belongs to force. As Jesus can never be thought of as a Roman soldier, so members of his church can never belong to the artillery, air force, or

---

[213] Eberhard Arnold, *The Early Christians after the Death of the Apostles*, (Ashton Keynes: Plough Publishing House, 1939), p. 4.

[214] Arnold, *The Early Christians*, pp. 16-17.

[215] Emmy, *Joyful Pilgrimage*, pp. 167-8.

[216] Arnold, *Innerland*, p. 202.

[217] Arnold, *Innerland*, p. 210.

police. Neither poison, bombs, pistols, or knives, neither the executioner's sword nor the gallows can be our weapon.'[218] Yet courageous spiritual battle was essential. Arnold observed: 'Equipped with the courage of the Holy Spirit, the church dares to do spiritual battle with all powers that withstand her love. All resistance of the present age is insignificant in her eyes. The Spirit, who guides and instructs her, is himself the utmost encouragement... The members of the church become his organs, for he pours the love of God into their hearts.'[219]

These themes are set out clearly in *Foundations*, which also adds other elements. In the section headed 'Our Calling', and under 'The Way of Peace', *Foundations* states: 'The way of peace demands reverence for all life, above all each human life, since every person is made in the image of God. Christ's word and example, as affirmed by the teaching of the early church, absolutely forbid us to take human life for any reason, directly or indirectly, whether in war or self-defense, through the death penalty, or by any other means, including euthanasia or abortion.' This takes in issues that Arnold did not address, but which have more recently been much discussed. *Foundations* writes in this way about war: 'As conscientious objectors, we will not serve in the armed services of any country, not even as noncombatants. Nor may we support war-making or the use of deadly force by others through our consent or aid.'[220] The position of the majority of the Anabaptists is clearly influential in the following statement: 'We refuse to wield governmental power by serving in high office or in any position such as judge or juror that is vested with power over the life, liberty, or civil rights of another. Likewise in obedience to Christ's teaching, we cannot swear oaths or make any pledge of allegiance. We love our country and our countrymen, but equally we love all our fellow human beings regardless of their nationality, ancestry, race, creed, culture, or social status. Our loyalty is to the kingdom of God.'[221]

Participation in government is an aspect of Bruderhof thinking on which Thomas Finger has commented. *Foundations* states that

---

[218] Arnold, *Innerland*, p. 227.

[219] Arnold, *Innerland*, p. 323.

[220] *Foundations*, p. 12.

[221] *Foundations*, p. 12.

community members are 'not indifferent to the work of government'. Finger asks whether the task of government might be perceived as 'creating and maintaining some degree of order and peace - not only protecting it by the sword, but also promoting it through laws, institutions, and services to benefit its people.' If so, he asks, could Christians work with and sometimes within governmental bodies? This is not the perspective of *Foundations*. In practice, Bruderhof members generally work in the community, many in producing 'Community Playthings' and Rifton Equipment industries, with others in schools and in publishing. *Foundations* sees the state as representing, at its best, 'a relative order of justice in the present sinful world; but the church, as God's embassy, represents an absolute order of justice: the righteousness of the kingdom of God. The church must witness to the state, serving as its conscience, helping it to distinguish good from evil, and reminding it not to overstep the bounds of its God-appointed authority.'[222] The community's way of peace is not seen as 'a pacifism of detachment or cowardice... Opposing war is only the first step; we seek to build up a life that removes the occasion for war by overcoming its root causes: injustice, hatred, and greed. We want to use our lives to advance the peaceable kingdom foretold by the prophets, which will transform not only individuals but also all human society and the whole of nature.'[223] This is a world-affirming spiritual vision.

Conclusion

The Bruderhof is a distinctive community with a distinctive spirituality. The movement has been the subject of study, but in much of the work that has been done the spirituality of the Bruderhof has not been the focus. There has been something of a tendency to look at the Bruderhof as a sociological phenomenon. Tyldesley comments that a writer such as Zablocki views Bruderhof identity in sociological terms and would see an account such as that by Merrill Mow, which portrays the history in spiritual terms, as quite inadequate.[224] The

---

[222] *Foundations*, p. 13.

[223] *Foundations*, p. 14.

[224] Tyldesley, *No Heavenly Delusion?*, p. 71. He also notes that the feeling would be mutual.

Bruderhof itself has to live with a degree of tension about its identity. On the one hand it sees itself as 'but a small part of what God – the God of Abraham, Isaac, and Jacob – has done through the ages'. Eberhard Arnold was willing to draw from many sources and this is true also of *Foundations*, which states: 'Right down to the present, wherever people strive for truth, justice, brotherhood, and peace, God is at work. We do not seek to imitate those who have gone before us; rather, we wish for their example to inspire us to live more wholeheartedly for God's kingdom.'[225] On the other hand, the Bruderhof has a very strong commitment to the very specific full community of goods, a practice that has not characterised most of those in the Anabaptist tradition. Thomas Merton described Arnold's advocacy in the 1920s of community as 'a fine gospel statement of community against the background of false community being spread in his day'.[226]

For Arnold, and for the contemporary Bruderhof, community itself is not enough. What is crucial is that Christian communities should be places where the Holy Spirit is at work. Thus Arnold wrote in *Innerland*: 'Inspired by the Easter message and the Pentecostal flame of the Holy Spirit, young people - "the holy springtime" - set out to consecrate new land to the church of the risen one.'[227] Here Arnold wanted to stress, as he often did, the radical spiritual movements that have characterised the history of the church. In similar vein, in 1928, he spoke about how the early Christians were followed in the second century by the radical movement, Montanism, and he wrote: 'The principle of life is essential to a living church; Christianity has nothing dead about it.'[228] Perhaps thinking of the parallels with the youth movement, Arnold noted that again and again, 'bands of awakened young people have set out. A hundred years after the first full community in Jerusalem, a new outpouring of the spirit of fire created the church again in Asia Minor.'[229] This move of the Spirit, in

[225] *Foundations*, p. 21.

[226] Thomas Merton, 'Building Community on God's Love', in Arnold, *Why We Live in Community*, p. 33.

[227] Arnold, *Innerland*, p. 277.

[228] Arnold, Meeting of the Bruderhof in November 1928, in *Brothers Unite*, pp. 11-12.

[229] Arnold, *Innerland*, p. 277.

Bruderhof spirituality, does not take place apart from the church – itself a 'sacrament', in the language of *Foundations*. Arnold wrote about the church receiving gifts from God: 'The church receives the power and authority to forgive sins through the power of his liberation. Jesus himself imparted it to her.'[230] Linked with this was the attitude to enemies. In July 1935 Arnold stated: 'Love for our enemies has to be so real that it reaches their hearts. For that is what love does.'[231] The Bruderhof has developed a strongly communal spirituality. With the help of the Holy Spirit, community members seek to live a biblically-orientated life of discipleship, following Christ together.

Appendix 1

Reference Number: Bruderhof Historical Archive, EA 25/15

Letter from Eberhard Arnold to his sister Hannah Arnold[232]

Sannerz, March 1925

Your letter is a very great joy to me, a most deeply felt joy, for I see from it that you are being and doing completely what God wants of you (as far as humanly possible), and what God has now led you to. I am with you wholeheartedly in your work; this I can be from the depths of my soul, for my long years of work building up the Fellowship and evangelizing have always been an essential part of my life, the life given me by God.

It is a misunderstanding, a totally false report, if you have been told that I ever expressed myself about the Fellowship or Revival Movement or its Christianity in such a way as to reject it. This has never been the case and never will be. I have never separated myself from the brothers and never will separate myself from them.

I can, however, understand how this erroneous opinion came about in regard to a leading that I know came to me from God. I have never expressed disapproval in the sense that the forgiveness of sins was being too strongly placed in the foreground. On the contrary, I am convinced that it is impossible to emphasize the forgiveness of sins too strongly. Life itself, God himself with His whole heart, is to be found in the

---

[230] Arnold, *Innerland*, p. 337.

[231] Arnold, *God's Revolution*, July 1935, p. 157.

[232] English translation by Bruderhof Historical Archives staff.

forgiveness of guilt--redemption from evil in the past as well as liberation from evil in the present.

What I do oppose energetically is something altogether different: when in spite of the experience of forgiveness of sins a person looks away from this great heart of God and gets enmeshed in his own small heart, becoming completely lost in his personal experience, his little personal self-life, and precisely in the religious sphere. A new self-life, an egotistical striving for personal purity, goodness, and happiness is then placed in the centre of religious experience; even work done for others is then done with an eye to one's own happiness. I am certain that it is because of the biblical prophets including John the Baptist and far more than all prophets--Jesus himself and his Holy Spirit that I am able to contradict this perversity.

Even so faithful a Fellowship Movement member as Fabianke calls it 'old and tired,' saying that 'new witnesses and new strength must be given to revive it' (*Warte* [a periodical], 1 March 1925, Supplement No.1). The cause of this tiredness is just this false subjectivity of the self-life, in which people devote themselves to their own little personal ego or that of their neighbour.

Basically this has always been recognized in the Fellowship Movement as well. Efforts were made to overcome it through an understanding of the Bible; the biblical prophecies of God's kingdom were studied a great deal. This is the way for all of us to become freer of Fellowship Christianity's tendency to a narrow focus on self; but as long as this understanding of the Bible remains merely intellectual, it has no power. As theory or dogma alone it is meaningless. Only when its living strength takes hold of our lives and transforms them to accord with God's kingdom does this understanding of the Bible become power and testimony.

Do sometime immerse yourself in the prophets and, in this connection, in Jesus' Sermon on the Mount. Just as it is impossible to emphasize the forgiveness of sins too strongly, so also is it impossible to emphasize God's kingdom and the Sermon on the Mount too strongly. In the all-encompassing words of the Sermon on the Mount, the character of God's rule and the character of the citizens of his kingdom are described very plainly--so plainly that we Christians of today are shown up as disobedient and faithless, as people who draw back from the great illuminating light of God's future.

In reality, however, Christ's church is appointed to conform to the character of this coming future. Forgiveness means the kingdom. God and his kingdom must become great in our lives so that we ourselves, including our private religious life, become small. To confess the greatness of God in his justice and holiness, in his all-inclusive love and mercy, to confess the greatness of God as Creator and Redeemer of the world -- that is the task of the church of God.

We all love the third chapter of John's Gospel, but we tend to forget that personal rebirth is here placed in the supra-personal context of the kingdom of God. The coming kingdom is the determining element in the Bible. It is this kingdom of the future that must overwhelm and completely fill us. The Holy Spirit wants to come over us and fill us in order to lead us into the future kingdom; the Spirit is to bring to life for us Jesus' words about the world of the future; the Spirit is to lead us toward this, so that we become a living example, a parable, a visible testimony of the coming kingdom.

You are right in saying that I, strongly moved by this kingdom of God and its future reality, have had close contact with many persons who had not yet been reborn in the biblical sense or were still very unclear in regard to this personal renewal. However, I never wanted to hold more strongly to those who were still outside God's kingdom than of those who are reborn and that stand at the service of God's kingdom.

All the same, I do question a rebirth that has no connection with God's coming kingdom; and I believe that God awakens many who open themselves to his coming kingdom but are still unclear about their personal forgiveness and sanctification. The evangelizing task devoted to people who truly hunger and are awakened by God must show us the way to see and acknowledge hunger for justice, thirst for God's love, and expectation of God's coming where they exist. We need to be given the strength to testify to the new birth from the Holy Spirit to those who are in this process of awakening, in the same way as Jesus spoke to Nicodemus, a man who was gripped by the kingdom like those in today's Youth Movement and the Religious Socialists. Equally however we must testify to Christians clearly and definitely--beginning with their personal lives--about their great responsibility in respect to the social justice of God's kingdom, in respect to Jesus Christ's coming kingdom of peace, and therefore in respect to the demands and promises of his Sermon on the Mount, just as Jesus did in a particular way to the group of his closest disciples.

You will understand then, Hannah, that I would be betraying my certainty before God if I were to say that the leading and work of the last years was a false way. I recognize that much of what I have done and put into effect in going this way was wrong and erroneous, just as you will recognize as wrong and erroneous many things on your way, that is, the way of purely personal Fellowship Christianity. All that I want to leave behind and overcome, and I trust in the power of the Holy Spirit, the power of the present Christ, that we may and can make a new start over and over again so that we can be more pure and undivided in following Christ, can follow him more devotedly and completely, and can represent God's coming kingdom. Yet for this very reason I must confess more than ever to the apparently new ways I have been led in the last years because I am convinced without any doubt that it is God who has led me on these ways and that he has done this for the sake of the witness of his kingdom and his Church.

It is obvious that there is a clear difference between the way of life of Fellowship Christianity as it has been till now on the one hand, and on the other the way of life community of work and community of goods, the religious-social proclaiming of God's kingdom to which we have been led and appointed. But more basic than this difference is the unity of the church between these different ways of life. There are many members, but one Body. The sense in which I hope to be regarded as a Fellowship Christian among other Fellowship Christians is the following: Christ demands of all believers that we recognize, testify, and prove the unity between all the forms of true discipleship and of the church in its biblical sense. This is more than any alliance, including the Blankenburg Alliance:[233] it is

---

[233] German Evangelical Alliance, based in Bad Blankenburg, Germany.

unity of the Body that is living in Christ, even if we do not recognize or acknowledge it.

We can draw on historical examples in the church and point to the fact that many were really in unity in the eyes of God and in the eyes of faith--the Lutherans and the Zwinglians, believing Catholics like Staupitz for example, the biblicist Schwenkfeldian movement of the Holy Spirit, the communistic peace churches of the Baptizers, and many other shadings of the Reformation era. This real unity existed in spite of the fact that, in their human blindness, they opposed and excluded one another, discovered human failings in each other, and repeatedly found grounds to accuse one another of heresy. There will soon be a similar historical situation in our day. No Christian wants to be one of those who one day, when their eyes are opened, will have to accuse themselves of denying the unity because of the differences. Among us who are living today the fulfilment of Jesus' plea must be revealed -- that they may all be one. By this unity, the wide world shall recognize that Jesus was sent by God.

This was the meaning of my request to you recently in Hamburg—and this is my request to you today: please help bring to expression this unity that exists in Christ, even though people deny it.

[Signed: Eberhard Arnold]